Contents

KT-424-450

Acknowledgements

We would like to thank the following for their support and for services provided.

Children and staff of Bradshaw County Primary School, Grappenhall, Warrington, for contributions to Chapters 9 and 10.

The British Orienteering Federation (see Chapter 4).

Kate Campion and members of Cheshire GEST 20-day primary geography course for the storybook list in Chapter 11.

Cathcart Primary School, Cole Street Primary School and Thingwall Junior School (Wirral LEA); and St Oswald's CE Primary School, Netherton (Sefton LEA), for work on the Developing Navigational Skills Project, relating to contributions to Chapter 4.

Stephanie Fearn, Headteacher, Beaconside CE Infants' School, Penrith, (Cumbria LEA), for contributions to Chapter 6.

The Elsie Talbot Bridge Trust, for financial support to the Geography INSET Primary Project.

Maureen Hollings, Wheelock County Primary School and Dorothy Nuttley, Winnington Park County Primary School, (Cheshire LEA), for ideas related to the use of literature in the classroom.

Wendy Horden, St Mary's CE Primary School, Rugeley (Staffordshire LEA) for contributions to Chapter 6.

Nicky Richardson, latterly of Cherry Trees School, Wombourn, Staffordshire, for contributions to Chapter 13.

Material with former Schools Council copyright is acknowledged (Chapter 2).

Silva (UK) Ltd (see Chapter 4).

The Sports Science Education Programme, administered on behalf of the Sports Council by the National Coaching Foundation (see Chapter 4).

Sue Walsh, Research Associate of the Developing Navigational Skills Project, for contributions to Chapter 4.

Windowgraphics, Southport, for much of the artwork.

Primary School Geography

Edited by

Bill Marsden and Jo Hughes

David Fulton Publishers Ltd
2 Barbon Close, London WC1N 3JX

First published in Great Britain by
David Fulton Publishers 1994

Note: The right of Bill Marsden and Jo Hughes to be identified as the editors of
this work has been asserted by them in accordance with the Copyright, Designs
and Patents Act 1988.

Copyright © David Fulton Publishers Limited

British Library Cataloguing in Publication Data

A catalogue record for this book is available from the British Library

ISBN 1-85346-281-0

Typeset by RP Typesetters, Unit 13, 21 Wren St, London WC1

Printed in Great Britain by BPC Books and Journals, Exeter

Preface

This book has been produced almost entirely by the members of the Steering Group of the Geography INSET Primary Project (GIPP), based in the Department of Education in the University of Liverpool. It is coedited by the project's Director, Professor Bill Marsden, and Associate Director, Jo Hughes. GIPP was established in 1990, with the support of Continuing Education funding, though over the last two years the project has had to rely largely on its own earnings.

Starting with school-based INSET, aimed at raising awareness of National Curriculum geography requirements in the primary school, the project has also run a considerable number of courses and conferences as part of the Department of Education's INSET programme. Among its publications are a series of *Guidesheets,* now distributed to a national mailing list of nearly 500, and a number of articles and inserts in *Primary Geographer.* In addition, the project team has contributed to publications produced by the North-west Consortium of five local education authorities (Cheshire, Cumbria, Lancashire, Shropshire and Staffordshire), for the Geographical Association and the National Curriculum Council. Its continuing work with the Consortium is most evident in the coordination of GEST-funded 20-day courses for primary geography teachers from the five authorities, the 1993 programme having attracted 141 participants.

The project is accountable to a Steering Group and it is its members (see page viii) who have been very largely responsible for the chapters in this volume. Only Andy Philips among the contributors is not a member of the Steering Group. The purpose of the book is to bring together the wide-ranging experience and expertise of the Group on a number of issues having a high degree of relevance in the implementation of geography, as one of the foundation subjects of the National Curriculum, in the primary school. It offers students and teachers – whether generalist, semi-specialist or specialist – knowledge, understanding and appreciation of geography's contribution to the curriculum of the primary school. Clearly the book's coverage cannot be comprehensive, but it seeks to deal with many of the issues which primary teachers currently have to address.

The first section offers recent and relevant historical context in the build-up to the National Curriculum. Chapter 1 exposes what John Dewey many years ago saw as the fallacy of polarising child-centred and subject-centred education as incompatible opposites, demonstrating that enquiry and activity-based work are the essence of good practice in both. Chapter 2 reinforces this thinking, drawing on the constructive synthesis of the Liverpool Schools Council 8–13 project of the 1970s which, like Dewey, saw geography and history, as well as integrated social sciences, as key resources for the primary curriculum. In Chapter 3, Wendy Morgan offers a unique contribution in the account of her involvement as the only primary teacher on the National Curriculum Geography Working Group, combined with an outline of the major contributions the Geographical Association has made to primary geography progress during the 1980s and 1990s, especially the journal, *Primary Geographer,* of which she is the founding editor.

In the second section, Chapter 4 is a firsthand account by Jim Martland of his Navigational Skills project, based in the Department of Education in the University of Liverpool, and the contribution it has made to a deeper understanding of the development of early mapping skills. Chapter 5 offers a case study of how a balanced and wide-ranging set of resources can readily be collected for an overseas locality study, while Chapter 6 presents two more case studies – in this event from two schools of contrasting type and location – of how the National Curriculum in geography has been implemented to date, drawing attention both to the opportunities and problems associated with this change. The final chapter of this second section presents a summary and checklists of good practice in assessment, as applied to primary geography, stressing that such practice cannot legitimately be detached from the general process of curriculum planning.

The third section of the book is particularly important in highlighting the many fruitful links between geography and other subjects and cross-curricular areas of the National Curriculum. In Chapter 8, Ashley Kent and Andy Philips draw on their long experience and range of contacts in offering a series of cameo studies of how information technology can naturally be permeated into primary geography. Similarly through case studies of different types, Bill Marsden in Chapter 9 and John Kenyon in Chapter 10 give examples of the range of fits between geography and other foundation and core subjects of the National Curriculum in focused topic work, not least in fieldwork. Jeremy Krause in Chapter 11 extends such links into studies of children's literature. Thus are established geography's connections not only with the science and humanities, but also with the aesthetic subjects. Chapter 12 explores the place of primary geography in the European dimension, while the final chapter surveys the ramifications of geography for special needs children.

When this book appears, the system will be set fair for post-Dearing changes. We have taken care that this book does not date as a result for, while addressing issues related to the implementation of the National Curriculum, its stress is on applying good practice in meeting the needs of that curriculum, and not on a mechanistic response to the superfluity of content demands in the pre-Dearing Orders, many of which will be swept overboard. At the same time, this book was written before the Dearing proposals were known, so that some of the pre-Dearing terminology has had to be retained. We are cautiously encouraged by what we have seen so far of Dearing's advice, as it relates to the primary phase. While on the face of it reducing the time available for geography, particularly at Key Stage 1, it:

(a) confirms its position in the National Curriculum;

(b) specifies it has access as a foundation subject to the 20% of time to be used at the school's discretion;

(c) asks that the content be arranged on a core plus options basis, adding flexibility to curriculum planning;

(d) confirms that geography will not be assessed by SATs and, perhaps, not even by formalised TAs, yet will have to be, as a minimum, formally reported on, on an annual basis, again adding flexibility;

(e) makes encouraging suggestions of linkages with other parts of the curriculum, to be established by Dearing's key stage groups, hopefully synthesising the suggestions of the concurrently active subject groups.

Our belief in the significance of geography as a resource and as a critical bridging subject (see Section 3) in the primary curriculum, is in essence not denied, and even is implicitly supported, in parts of the Dearing proposals. At the same time, there is the risk that some schools will concentrate on the narrower aspects of Dearing and adopt a utilitarian lowest-common-denominator approach that would return us to the type of curriculum heavily criticised in the HMI reports of the late 1970s and early 1980s. It is our hope that this volume may help to contribute rather to a highest-common-factor approach.

List of Contributors

Ray Derricott is Director of Continuing Education in the University of Liverpool, and was Co-director of the Liverpool Schools Council 8–13 Project, as described in Chapter 2. Apart from the many publications associated with the Project, he is the editor of *Curriculum Continuity – Primary to Secondary,* and co-author of *The Social Significance of Middle Schools.*

Jo Hughes was formerly Environmental Education coordinator at Kew Woods Primary School, Southport, and is now Associate Director of GIPP. Apart from contributions to *Primary Geographer,* she is a co-author of the Geographical Association's *Ladakh* pack, and also of the *Ginn Geography* primary series.

Ashley Kent is Senior Lecturer in Geographical Education and Geography Coordinator at the University of London Institute of Education. He has produced a wide range of publications for the Geographical Association, several of which have concerned information technology. He is the co-author of a number of well-known texts, including the *Oxford Geography Project* and, most recently, *Understanding Human Geography: People and their Changing Environments.* He has a long-standing interest in curriculum development, mainly inspired by his former position as Associate Director of the Geography 16–19 Project.

John Kenyon is Headteacher of Bradshaw County Primary School, Grappenhall, Warrington. He has worked closely over recent years with GIPP and also with a major science education project (CRIPSAT) based in the University of Liverpool's Department of Education. He is a member of the Geographical Association's Education Standing Committee.

Jeremy Krause is Cheshire LEAs Geography Adviser. He is co-author of a forthcoming book *Geography 5 to 11,* and of a number of publications for the Geographical Association. He plays an active role in the Geographical Association, serving on its Council, Primary Geography Advisory Group, Geography Advisers' and Inspectors' Group, and its Education Standing Committee.

Bill Marsden is Professor of Education in the University of Liverpool, and Director of GIPP. He has produced a large number of articles and contributions to books on primary geography and on the history of the curriculum, and is author of *Evaluating the Geography Curriculum,* and co-author of the *Oliver and Boyd Geography* primary series. He is a Council member and Publications Officer of the Geographical Association, and President of its Liverpool and District branch.

Jim Martland is Lecturer in Education at the University of Liverpool and was for twelve years Director of the Primary PGCE course. Since 1989 he has directed a research project on the navigational skills of young children, sponsored by the Sports Council and the British Orienteering Federation. Among the many publications of this project is his co-authored *Using the Silva Model 7DNS Compass* and *Orienteering in the National Curriculum.*

Wendy Morgan was a primary school headteacher and a member of the National Curriculum Geography Working Group. She is well-known as Honorary Editor of the Geographical Association's highly successful journal for teachers, *Primary Geographer.* Her many publications include planning booklets for the Geographical Association, and resources featuring St Lucia and Flatford of which she is co-author. Adviser to the Ginn primary geography team, she co-authored teachers' materials for Key Stage 1 Geography. She serves on the Geographical Association's Council and other committees.

Keith Paterson is Principal Lecturer and Head of the Department of European Studies at the Liverpool Institute of Higher Education. He was a member of the National Curriculum Geography Working Group and is Chair of the GIPP Steering Group. Currently involved with curriculum and exchange developments in Europe, his publications relate to physical and environmental issues, information technology and the curriculum. He is co-author of the Geographical Association's *Ladakh* pack.

Andy Philips is Senior Lecturer in Education at St Mary's College, Strawberry Hill. Prior to this he was National Coordinator of HIT (Humanities and Information Technology), and is senior co-editor of the Longman/Project HIT publications. He has also produced many articles on geography and information technology.

David Thomas is Senior Lecturer in Education at the University of Liverpool, and was until recently Director of its Department of Education's INSET unit. For many years he also directed the Department's special needs provision. His publications include *The Social Psychology of Childhood Disability,* and *The Experience of Handicap.*

PART A

Contexts

CHAPTER 1

Places and Peoples: Continuity and Change in Primary Geography

Bill Marsden

The Place of Geography in the Primary Curriculum: Enquiry into the Local Locality

Generalist primary teachers, especially those in the infant phase, have long been concerned about the place of 'subjects' in the primary curriculum. This concern has been intensified by the choice of a subject framework for the National Curriculum. Many have been conditioned by the view, supposedly emerging from the Hadow and Plowden reports which officially supported a progressive ideology, that subject teaching is antipathetic to child-centred learning. The purpose of this chapter is to suggest that there is no built-in incompatibility between good primary practice and good subject practice, in this case as related to geography.

To show that this is not merely the lobbying of a geography specialist, I draw on evidence not from geographers making the claim, but from progressive educational thinkers over the past sixty years or so. Let us start with the Hadow Report of 1932. As the first example in the history of English education to provide official support for progressive ideas, it did not at the same time, as its disciples later were prone to do, polarise primary practice and subject practice. It stated boldly that:

> 'Work in the primary school *in geography,* as in other subjects, must "be thought of in terms of activity and experience rather than of knowledge to be acquired and facts to be stored" '. (p.171)

At the same time it did not deny that there were 'certain geographical facts' which 'must be learned'. But these had to be a means to an end, not acquired for their own sakes but 'connected with known realities'. Children should not be taught things that they could not understand. In the infant school, the input of geography should be integrated with the more general teaching, 'before this is differentiated into subjects at a later stage', i.e. about the age of nine. Much advice was given on the type of geography that should be included, whether in the integrated framework lower down, or in the more systematic geography provision higher up in the junior phase. Good practice was therefore based on providing an activity or enquiry-basis for learning. The argument was not against geography as such, but the narrow notetaking and recall in the examinations tradition that became associated with the grammar schools.

About the time of the Hadow Report, the tutor in geographical education at the Froebel Educational Institute Training College was Olive Garnett. She wrote a methodological text, *Fundamentals in School Geography,* intended as a guide for teachers and students in training. First published in 1934, it was reprinted during and after the second World War.

Following Hadow, Garnett stressed the importance of progressive methods, including outdoor observation and exploration and, in the school, activity-based work within an integrated timetable. But she was equally clear about the importance of maintaining a genuinely geographical input:

> '...from the age of about seven upward, the interests of children frequently lead them to pursue topics that are partly or even largely geographical. Children also come to feel the need for some of the geographical tools and materials, especially maps. The substance of modern geography, at least at the school stage, is very close to everyday life and to the interests of children. Any junior school programme based on children's interests is likely to devote more time than formerly to work that is geographical, although there may be nothing called 'geography' in the timetable. It is therefore no less desirable than hitherto that junior school teachers should be aware of the nature and standards of geography, although they may not teach the subject as such.' (p.3)

Garnett's conclusion was that geography as a separate subject should not appear on the junior timetable for children below the age of nine, as

Hadow had suggested. At the same time, she was firm that teachers and children of all ages should be made aware of what was good geography: the 'geography of geographers' (p.20). Though they might not know it as geography, 'nothing but the real thing, scientific truth, should be offered to children of any age.' She made explicit the approach that should be followed: it was the research approach.

> 'Fantastic though the suggestion may at first appear, there is a similarity between the methods of geographical research and the activities of children who have opportunity to pursue certain interests which come naturally to them.' (Garnett, 1940, p.171)

For younger children, such geographical-type research obviously meant firsthand observation and investigation out of doors through local study. This followed the precepts of the time-honoured *heimatskunde* tradition. One problem of this approach was that it had become associated with the view that only rural or rural-type studies in parks were suitable for primary fieldwork. The desirability of getting 'back to nature' was seen to be vital to the physical, social and moral well-being of the urban child. Most schools were, however, in towns, in environments from which the children needed protection. Opportunely, in 1938 Cons and Fletcher's *Actuality in School: an Experiment in Social Education,* addressed the importance of work in the school locality, whether rural or urban.

> '...actuality in education is concerned with the use of the environment, because, in fact, the child's environment is the range of his own experiences. Within this are the things he sees, the people he comes in contact with every day, the shops where he buys his food...and the streets along which he walks. So that actuality in education involves bringing the child into conscious and direct touch with the various aspects of the life of the community.' (p.8)

Once more progressive primary thinking reinforced the ideas of pioneering geographical educators, in showing that the first approach to enquiry or research-based learning was through fieldwork in the home locality, wherever it might lie.

'Distant Places and Peoples'

While home-based enquiry was the starting point, one problem of progressive education was that, in its justifiable emphasis on activity and experience, it tended to regard the direct experience as the only countable experience, in effect the finishing point, for young children. As the archetypal twentieth century progressive, John Dewey (1916) argued, however, it was the role of geography in the primary curriculum

4

to 'bring about the enlargement of the significance of direct experience', providing, with history, 'the most direct and interesting roads out into the larger world of meaning'. (pp.210–3) Once more, a leading progressive voice had reinforced the view of the geographical educationalist of the subject's importance as a global study.

HMI reports on the state of the art in primary geography in the 1970s and 1980s were generally critical, but less of local study work than of the more wide-ranging elements of geography. This chapter will therefore concentrate on an area the inspectors saw as less well-covered, yet a central part of geography's distinctive contribution to the curriculum. This relates to moving out from the locality and the home region into the larger world of more distant places.

The study of distant places and peoples introduces another dimension however. It is possible for the work to be sound in terms of geographical content and progressive teaching methods, but to be unsound so far as social education is concerned. Thus, despite the excellence of most of her guidance, Olive Garnett was a person of her time in her commitment to the notion that being a citizen of the British Empire was a contribution to becoming a good citizen of the world. 'Children of this country will become citizens of the world in ways that are more apparent than is the case for citizens of some other countries...' (pp.16–7), apparently because of Britain's special world role derived from its wide-ranging trade and imperial contacts.

In her advice to teachers and students, Garnett identified a number of textbook series published in the 1930s that were of service in offering up-to-date materials on 'people and homes of many lands'. One of the series was the *New Age Geographies,* interesting in being co-authored by a primary specialist, Elsa Stamp, and her husband, Sir Dudley Stamp, one of the most eminent geographers of his time.

Though the series contains a number of anachronisms, and to an extent was patronising in its tone, it followed many aspects of good practice in terms of pedagogy, geography and social education. Thus each section:

(a) started with familiar things, such as day-to-day food and clothes, and led out from these to their origins in the wider world; or,
(b) had 'named' fictional characters, Tom, Dick and Harry and their female counterparts, about to embark on some journey round the world, by land, air or sea, in effect a story-book method aimed at motivating children, enhancing global knowledge, and giving a sense of places, people and their ways of life;
(c) contained geographical material that was authentic not least because Dudley Stamp was an inveterate traveller, who took and used his own

photographs. By the standards of its time, the series was impressive in emphasising that good geography was based on:

— the real world;
— visual materials as well as maps;
— cultural interests associated with distant places;
— the importance of simulated travel;
— the involvement of children as well as adults on the 'great world stage';
— the global context of the subject.

Unlike many contemporary textbooks, the series was less concerned with emphasising the imperial heritage and with studies of exotic primitive peoples. Indeed the Stamps were scathing about the 'simple peoples' approach, regarding the Eskimos, for example, as 'too unimportant' to be given attention, and also as being inaccurately presented (as they continue to be) when they were given attention.

'Only 5 per cent of Eskimos are familiar with snow houses; half of them have never heard of such a dwelling. It is true 45 per cent have heard of them, but then they have learned geography in English-speaking schools.' (pp.v–vi)

The perception that a central purpose of school geography was the study of distant lands and their peoples created a tension between good pedagogy and good social education. It brought with it the problem of unfavourable stereotyping. An exotic approach to simple peoples was seen as particularly entertaining for young children. The tensions can be explored through one of the most famous series of its time, that by A.B. Archer and Helen Thomas, entitled *Geography: First Series,* intended to introduce children to geography in a friendly, informal way. First published in the 1930s, the series was still in print over thirty years later. It was accompanied by a methodological text by Helen Thomas, entitled *Teaching Geography.*

From the standpoint of good pedagogy, the Archer and Thomas series is hard to fault. It was graded in terms of language and size of print. In the first book the unit headings were the names of real children, like Tooktoo the Eskimo boy and Hirfa the Bedouin girl, while in later ones generalisations like 'the nomad lands', and 'lands of scattered settlements' were used. By the technical standards of the time the presentation was exemplary, with many large and clear visual materials, 'bringing the world into the classroom'. From the start, probing 'why'-type questions were integrated with the text, requiring indirect observation and interpretation of photographs. The realities of photographs were introduced before the abstractions of maps.

The aim of the series was above all to provoke interest in the world by seeing it through the eyes of children in distant places, thus humanising the approach. It was recognised that it was important to acquire locational knowledge, but this was to be done as a means to an end. More important was the development of reasoning powers and, beyond this of 'cultural enrichment of the mind and training for intelligent citizenship', including the elimination of racial and national prejudice. 'Many national problems are rooted in provincialism', wrote Thomas (1940, pp.8–13) in a handbook to the series, and indeed it was unusual in starting with distant places.

To this end, the children found in the first book of the series are presented in a favourable light, unlike the blatantly negative stereotypes of other texts in the inter-war years, like the 'indescribably repulsive...hideous' pygmies, giving off 'an extraordinarily inescapable blend of stenches' of another series (Schebesta, 1933, pp.25–6). What then, were the problems posed by the series on the criteria of good social education? One point is that the children were generally stereotyped, as were those in most other texts, as happy and problem-free (Wright, 1983).

> 'The children of the Congo have no toys like yours, but they are happy just the same. They run and jump and play games, and have just as much fun as you do.' (Archer and Thomas, 1936, p.16)

Thus the impression is left of simple tropical peoples with lesser needs than their European counterparts. Similarly, the presentation emphasises the exotic, albeit less so in Archer and Thomas than in other series. Here there is a genuine emphasis on interaction of peoples and their environments, promoting a sense of skilled though simple human adjustments. While the environment itself is not presented in such hostile terms as in other texts of the time, at the same time there are undertones of tropical indolence (with Tooktoo's Eskimo people having to work harder than Bombo's, for example) and dangerous animal stereotypes, with crocodiles lurking on every river bank 'ready to make a meal of anyone who is unlucky enough to fall in the river.'

In terms of social education therefore, Archer and Thomas presented what was in fact a somewhat romanticised world, cocooning young children from the harsher realities of poverty and the exploitation present in Britain's and in other empires. The series, despite being more sensitive than most of its time, implicitly supported the status quo. An issues-orientation was lacking.

More formal advocacy of what were in effect detailed if simulated case studies was a feature of the journals and methodological texts of the 1950s. They were referred to at that time as 'sample studies' (Hickman, 1950). A balanced coverage of the world through sample studies, integrated into a course book, was seen as more consumer-friendly and as avoiding what had long become rigid and mechanistic regional geography approaches, particularly unsuited to the primary school.

As the sixties and seventies progressed, sample studies became more issues-orientated, at secondary level at least. They were now referred to as case studies. A welfare approach to geographical study became increasingly influential. This can be seen in the advocacy of the Liverpool Schools Council 8–13 project, to be considered in the next chapter. At the primary level, children (or perhaps their teachers) were still regarded as requiring protection from controversy and the fact that the world was not a particularly happy place. In dichotomising child-centred and society-centred education, the progressive primary ideology bypassed the urgent need to provide for the child a global dimension from an early age (Alexander, 1984).

Such polarisation is often blamed on the Plowden Report of 1967. This Report was in fact a much better balanced document than is often presented. If read through at firsthand, rather than interpreted from selected quotes, it is seen to reinforce the views of Hadow and Garnett and support the basic argument of this chapter, that there is not an intrinsic incompatibility between topic and subject approaches. It also addressed the point that children should be guided early into worlds beyond the home and school area.

The Plowden Report clearly reinforced the notion that subject timetabling is inappropriate for younger children, though it accepted that conventional subjects became more relevant towards the top of the junior school. It included four pages of densely packed advice on how geography might be integrated into good primary practice. In particular it approved the use of 'sample studies' of distant places which 'carry much of the authenticity of local geography and permit comparisons to be made with the home region', helping to lead outwards from local studies to areas that could not be visited.

Looking forward, such thinking is in turn enshrined in National Curriculum geography, within the framework of 'locality studies', an alternative title to sample or case studies. Looking back, the Plowden arguments were anticipated by earlier progressives, not least of them, John Dewey. His view leads naturally into the next chapter, where a differentiated notion of the potential value of geography in the primary curriculum is carried foward in an account of the work in this field of the Liverpool Schools Council Project of the 1970s. The critical points

Dewey (1916) emphasised are to be found in the following:

> 'The residence, pursuits, successes and failures of men are the things that give the geographic data their reason for inclusion...The earth as the home of man is humanizing and unified; the earth viewed as a miscellany of facts is scattering and imaginatively inert. Geography is a topic that originally appeals to the imagination...It shares in the wonder and glory that attach to adventure, travel and exploration. The variety of peoples and environments, their contrast with familiar scenes, furnishes infinite stimulation. The mind is moved from the monotony of the customary. And while local or home geography is the natural starting point...it is an intellectual starting point for moving out into the unknown, not an end in itself...when the familiar fences that mark the limits of the village proprietors are signs that introduce an understanding of the boundaries of great nations, even fences are lighted with meaning.' (pp.211–2)

What is positive about the National Curriculum is that by making geography statutory it protects primary children from the idiosyncrasies of individual school planning, some of which offered little geography but much history, and vice versa. Many children prior to the 1990s were denied the entitlement of the geographical contribution to a broad and balanced curriculum.

A negative element in the National Curriculum in geography is that it has stepped back from dealing with controversial issues and the promotion of international understanding. Dewey would have seen through the nationalistic undertones. But it does subscribe to the following features of good geography practice and good primary practice.

• It actively promotes linkages between places, themes and skills, the essence of geographical study.
• It offers many opportunities of linking with other curricular areas and cross-curricular themes.
• It does not dictate a subject-based timetable: a topic framework is still possible, though it does need to be more focused than in the past.
• For Key Stages 1 and 2 in particular, the programmes of study indicate that enquiry-based approaches should be followed.

To quote the first paragraph of the Programme of Study for Key Stage 1 (1991):

> 'Work should be linked to the pupils' own interests, experience and capabilities and should lead to investigations based on both fieldwork and classroom activities. Much of pupils' learning in Key Stage 1 should be based on direct experience, practical activities and exploration of the local area.' (p.31)

It is not all that different from the earlier quotation from the Hadow Report.

CHAPTER 2

Subjects as Resources: From a Schools Council Project to National Curriculum Geography

Ray Derricott

The Schools Council for Curriculum and Examinations came into being at October 1964. It must be noted that in the full, official title, Curriculum came before Examinations, winning an important debate, at least in a symbolic way, that curricular matters should take precedence over assessment and examinations. The curriculum, it was thought, should not be assessment-led (Plaskow, 1985; Manzer, 1970). The contrast with the Education Reform Act of 1988 is strong. In 1988, the National Curriculum Council was clearly separated from the Schools Examinations and Assessment Council both functionally and geographically – the former being located in York and the latter in London. However, the two organisations had been merged by 1993. Either separately or merged, the Councils remain peopled by ministerial nomination. By sharp contrast, in the 1960s the Schools Council had a committee structure which represented the partners – the DES, the LEAs and teachers. In most committees teachers were in the majority. The major function of the Schools Council was not to prescribe to schools what ought to be done but to widen the choices of ideas and materials that were available to teachers. Thus in the 1960s, in an economic climate which was relatively warm, and resources available for growth within the educational system, teachers were offered opportunities to take a central role in the reconstruction and development of the curriculum. The period from the mid-sixties to the mid-seventies saw these opportunities squandered, as within the Schools Council itself priorities for development never effectively emerged, and amongst teachers, misunderstanding and mistrust of the Council's efforts grew. It is no wonder that in the cold economic climate of the 1980s and a very difficult political climate teachers found themselves dispirited, and lacking in confidence. With the erosion of public support and being generally disorganised as a profession, teachers were in no condition to resist the accelerating pace of central control over the content and control of the curriculum which took place throughout the decade of the eighties and culminated in the Education Reform Act of 1988 and the development of Statutory Instruments for subjects. Although the early 1990s have seen signs of organised opposition to central dictates, especially those relating to national assessment programmes, there is little doubt that the fundamental position has changed since the era of the Schools Council.

It has been necessary to paint the above backcloth, no matter how sketchy, in order to begin the analysis of the place of geography in the primary curriculum during the period of the burgeoning of large national projects in the pre- and post-Plowden period from 1965 to 1976.

The Plowden Report is often thought to have been the most influential statement of the epitome of progressivism as applied to primary education. It was seen as an expression of child-centred education (1967) and has often been blamed for what some writers saw as the falling of standards and the neglect of the basic subjects (Baker, 1987) and which politicians and writers from the radical right of the 1980s saw as the justification of educational reform and which in turn led to the 1988 Act and the National Curriculum (Scruton, 1991).

A more detailed study of the Plowden Report will reveal its child-centredness and no more so than in the famous sentence:

'At the heart of the educational process lies the child' (Plowden Report, para. 9, p.7).

The Report of 1967, in terms of ideology, is not much more than a restatement of the values that permeate the Hadow Report of 1931. In terms of teaching and learning these values are typically laid down in the following:

'At the age when they attend the primary schools, children are active and inquisitive, delighting in movement, in small tasks that they can perform with deftness and skill, and in the sense of visible and tangible accomplishment...These activities are not aimless, but form the process by which children grow' (Board of Education, Hadow Report, 1931, p.xv).

However, although both reports see knowledge for young children being a seamless robe they both make particular reference to the importance of subjects. Both reports have sections on geography (see Chapter 1) and provided significant frameworks and guidelines for the teaching of geography for those teachers who took the time to study them. The reports hinted strongly at notions of sequencing of content and matching teaching ideas and concepts to individual development. It was possible for informed geographers and teachers to build a syllabus from such guidance. Many published school texts followed these guidelines and increased their sales.

It was against this background that in 1971 the Schools Council funded the project History, Geography and Social Science in the Middle Years of Schooling, 8–13. This rather long, cumbersome title was eventually shortened to either HGSS or Place, Time and Society. However, the longer title was the product of the debates which had taken place in the Schools Council about the nature of the shape and style of the curriculum in the area of the social subjects. In the late 1960s and early 1970s there had been much discussion about the development of a notion of the Middle Years of Schooling usually taken as the education of children between ages 8 and 13.

It had been argued that the middle years taken as a whole should represent the coming together of the primary tradition and the secondary tradition (Schools Council, 1969, and Blyth and Derricott, 1977). The curricular experiences of children should be continuous and guided by the same principles, no matter what kind of school in which they received their schooling. The new Middle Schools, either for 8–12, 9–13 or 10–13 year olds, were designed to bridge the passage from primary to secondary education. In practice, the primary and secondary traditions proved in many cases to be difficult to bridge. Some middle schools, no matter for which age group they catered, became 'hinged' schools with practices in the lower part of the schools remaining primary in nature and the upper schools becoming secondary in nature (Nias, 1985).

Where did Geography figure in this debate? The brief given to the HGSS Project Team by the Schools Council in the first half of the 1970s was, in part, to provide some answers to the question posed above. The HGSS Project was to develop ideas and teaching materials to support the teaching of History, Geography and Social Science in the middle years, whether the subjects were considered 'separately or in combination'. This latter phrase was chosen to encourage the project team to explore the nature of curricula which were organised under broad areas.

Geography in the middle years, at that time, was being used or ignored in the plethora of organisational devices, each with its particular bands of supporters, which operated under such labels as Environmental Studies, Social Studies, Urban Studies, Integrated Studies, Cultural Studies, and Humanities. Members of the Schools Council Geography Subject Committee, one of the three powerful groups within the Council, who were sponsoring the HGSS Project, were keen to maintain the integrity of geography within the Middle Years Curriculum.

The HGSS Project Team was appointed to represent a microcosm of this debate. The six-strong team contained well-qualified historians, geographers and social scientists, all of whom also being experienced teachers of children in the middle years. The debate within the team was long, sharp and critical, with representatives of each discipline having to defend their ground whilst still seeking a basis upon which they could plan together a curriculum for the social subjects for the middle years. This was also taking place at the height of the philosophical debates about the nature of the logic of the curriculum being led by Hirst and Peters (Hirst, 1975, Peters, 1969) and the sociological debate about curricular paradigms led by Bernstein (1975).

The diagram below represents the basic position of the HGSS Project about the distinctions between disciplines and school subjects.

Figure 2.1

are resources available for the teaching of

| **The social disciplines of** |
| History, Geography, Economics, Sociology, Social Anthropology, Social Psychology and Political Science |

in the study of

the **social subjects either**	
separately history, geography, separate social sciences	**or together** social studies, environmental studies, humanities, integrated studies

(Blyth, et al., 1976)

| **Man in Place, Time and Society** |

Using this model, geography is seen as a resource available to teachers in approaching their curriculum planning and in developing appropriate, related teaching and learning experiences for their pupils. The idea of geography as a resource is an apparently simple idea but then in the 1970s and probably now in the 1990s, it is a difficult message to communicate effectively to teachers. The apparently simple message has a number of nuances attached to it.

1 Geography as a discipline as studied in higher education differs from geography as a school subject. There may be times when discipline and subject are close to each other in focus and at other times the two might be separated by large and significant gaps. The geography described in the Hadow Report of 1931 and the Plowden Report of 1967 differed little except for a prominence in the latter report given to the acquisition of related language skills. Both reports described geography as a school subject. Working in 1976 (Blyth et al., 1976) the HGSS team noted the changes in academic geography which were taking the discipline nearer to those of the social sciences in seeking ways of trying to explain and to predict what happens in particular locations. The danger of concentrating on this process added to the risk of the discipline retreating into 'statistical impersonality' (Blyth et al., 1976).

Even by the mid-1970s the HGSS Project recognised that some teachers were moving their emphases to reflect the changes in geography as a discipline. The main publication of HGSS noted:

'...if Geography in its modern form is looked upon as a subject resource, then it has a great deal to offer along with other disciplines in respect of skills, techniques and insights' (Blyth et al., 1976, p.43).

2 Changes in academic disciplines that have potential for use in schools need communicating effectively to teachers who wish to use the new ideas. Teachers need constantly updating on changes and trends within disciplines. For primary and middle school teachers who may have few qualifications in geography, their in-service needs become greater. In this sense, the HGSS Project became a teacher in-service education project. Project conferences and workshops for teachers were teaching geography as well as exploring teaching techniques appropriate for new teaching materials.

As a resource, what had geography to offer to children and to teachers? The HGSS Project claimed that geography as a resource could offer children of primary school age, firstly, relevance to their own lives. Working with both teachers and children the Schools Council Project discovered that teachers often underestimate children's ability to explore geographical situations in which they were encouraged to look for **similarities** and **differences.**

Secondly, geography offered many realistic situations in which children and teachers together could explore the **values** of different groups. For example, issues within the environment from litter, noise, pollution, land use and control of the use of cars in city centres are just a few themes through which the values of groups and individuals can be explored. The HGSS Project was not intent to teach a particular set of values but to encourage teachers and children to engage in the process of **valuing.** Geography, as a resource, was a fertile subject in providing subject material for this process.

Thirdly, the HGSS Project emphasised the development of **critical thinking.** The encouragement of **collecting** and **evaluating** evidence was one of the project's most significant objectives. Geography provides plenty of instances in which critical thinking can be exercised. The use of critical thinking means challenging statements, assumptions and habits of thought and belief. For young children, key questions in this respect are:

Is this statement really true?

How do we know? What is the evidence?

Why are things always done this way?

Why do these people or individuals think that something is important? In asking questions in this way, children can also be encouraged to exercise **empathy** which was another of the HGSS Project objectives.

Fourthly, as a resource, geography can be used to develop **a readiness to think in terms of spatial distributors.** The Project Team put this as follows.

'Some people regard the mapping aspect of spatial competence as a rather trivial matter, but there is an important difference between the mere acquisition of mapwork skills and the use of maps as a means of formulating new hypotheses and ideas'. (Blyth et al., 1976, p.46).

Finally, geography as a resource can be used effectively to develop in children a material, European or a **global perspective.** In this way local problems or issues can be seen as occurring globally. For example, poverty in the Third World is a global responsibility.

Geography as a resource therefore has a major place in the primary curriculum. However, one of the problems faced by the HGSS Project was how to communicate this message effectively to teachers. Many primary school teachers in the 1970s (and probably also today) were uneasy with their own lack of knowledge and the uncertainty of introducing new approaches to teaching which had a strong implicit message for changing the nature of relationships between teacher and the taught.

In this approach to teaching geography, both teachers and their pupils were having to learn how to cope with uncertainty. In many of the topics, there were no single answers and often the most appropriate answer was: 'we do not know'. To some teachers this approach undermined their confidence and threatened the security they felt in their classrooms. Often teachers agreed that the objectives and ideas being advocated by the HGSS Project were far too sophisticated for young children. It was also agreed that many of the ideas being advocated by the project were adult ideas which were being imposed upon children who were often not ready for these ideas either emotionally or intellectually. The HGSS Project Team demonstrated on many occasions that children of primary school age could cope with geographical ideas if they were taught in a classroom or group climate which cultivated an emotional ethos in which individuals were encouraged to offer their own ideas and explanations. Even these were often incomplete, but were given careful consideration in an intellectual ethos where teachers and children explored ideas together, and were prepared to cope with the uncertainty which often surrounds the issues being studied. The Project Team took the position taken by Bruner that any idea from an academic discipline can be taught with integrity and meaning to learners of any age.

The HGSS Project believed that as children moved through the primary and middle years of schooling they should be led to discover some of the important concepts, categories and organising structures of subjects. Thus at some time during the middle years children should experience geography as geography and history as history.

This raises the problem of progression through this process. The HGSS team represented this in the following way.

Figure 2.2

PRE-DISCIPLINARY ACTIVITIES............................DISCIPLINARY ACTIVITIES
    CONTRIVED EXPERIENCES
    CONTROLLED VARIABLES

        coping with uncertainty
        encouraging opinion sharing
        encouraging judgement making
        coping with conflicting evidence or opinions
        detecting bias
                          USE OF CASE STUDY
                          MATERIAL FROM HISTORY,
                          GEOGRAPHY OR
                          SOCIAL SCIENCES

(Derricott and Blyth, 1979)

Figure 2.2 represents the model used by the HGSS Project to suggest strategies for introducing ideas from geography during the primary years. The first task facing teachers is to identify a starting point at which any interaction with young children can begin. As Ausubel (1968) has indicated, the most important single factor influencing learning is what the learner already knows.

The first assumption made by the HGSS team was that children in early years are unlikely to know any formal geography. A distinction was therefore made between **pre-disciplinary** and **disciplinary activities.** Pre-disciplinary activities have, as their basis, common sense knowledge which figures already in children's cognitive maps. Starting points are events from everyday life with which children may already have some familiarity.

These activities cannot be classified as geography but are carefully chosen for the opportunities they provide for children to practise the skills valued by subject specialists. Disciplinary activities, on the other hand, are drawn from the traditional content of geography. The aim of the teaching strategy is to provide a progression of activities (and of learning) from pre-disciplinary to disciplinary. The progression involves, in the early stages, the use of contrived experiences in which variables are controlled before the introduction of actual case study material with a disciplinary focus.

The strategies encourage:
— coping with the uncertainty of not knowing;
— coping with the fact that there is no single 'correct' answer to a problem;
— sharing opinions;
— making judgements;
— distinguishing between facts and opinions;
— coping with conflicting evidence;
— detecting bias in evidence.

Similar strategies were advocated to encourage the exercising of empathy. Both these strategies, with teaching examples, can be found in Derricott and Blyth (1979).

To this point most of the ideas of the HGSS Project have dealt with teaching geography separately from the other social subjects. Another important brief given to the project was to investigate ways of teaching the subjects of history, geography and the social sciences in combination. In order to do this, the project advocated the use of a planning framework which used **key concepts.** Key concepts are high levels of abstraction which contain the potential for helping teachers to plan and to teach themes and issues by using the social subjects in an interrelated way. This theme could be planned and taught, for example, using ideas and content from both history and geography so that the integrity of the separate subjects was maintained.

The project's list of **key concepts** were:

— similarity/difference
— continuity/change
— communication
— power
— values and belief
— conflict/consensus
— causes and consequences.

The seven key concepts were not presented as an exhaustive list. Neither was the list exclusive to the social subjects; nor was it claimed to have any epistemological nor philosophical status. In the judgement of the Project Team, the key concepts were thought to be useful to teachers in grading selection and organisation of content whether the social subjects were being planned to be taught separately or in combination.

The HGSS Project Team did not claim that primary school children would attain a high level of understanding of the key concepts. It was not intended that children should learn by rote definitions of the key concepts. However, it was claimed that if children are subject to the kinds of questions that the key concepts provoke, and experiences are structured with the key concepts in mind, they will begin on the road to understanding and using these concepts.

Key concepts were (and still are) remote ideas to many teachers who, in turn, see these concepts as even more remote from young children. This was the greatest problem the HGSS Project faced in communicating its ideas to teachers and it is the writer's view that this level of communication was low and often ineffective. However, the project did offer some guidelines to teachers in the use of key concepts.

Figure 2.3, on page 18, represents the model used for this guidance. Because there was no adequate conceptual map for teaching the social subjects available in the 1970s (and little progress has been made on this into the 1990s), the model is a postulation. Although the learning of concepts is not thought to be linear but is likely to be highly complex, the simple model assumes three levels of concepts which can be seen as hierarchical. At **Level I** are the hundreds or even thousands of **specific concepts** that are used by historians, geographers and social scientists. Some examples of these might be war, army, costume, uniform, money, market, site, transport, route, path, mountain, valley, etc. Concepts at Level I are relatively easy to define, narrow in scope, can be experienced

18

Figure 2.3

Criteria for assessing the appropriateness of concepts for children 7–13

Type of concept	Criteria	Distance from child's experience	Complexity	Scope concept	Open endedness	AGE
Specific concepts	Level I	Directly related	Can be experienced through senses	Narrow in scope	Closed and easy to define	7
Sub-ordinate concepts	Level II					
Key concepts	Level III	Unrelated	Abstract notion	Broad in scope	Open to disagree-ment about interpreta-tion and meaning	13

(Elliott, 1979)

through the senses or through vicariously evoked experiences using language, movement and drama.

At **Level II** are **subordinate concepts.** These are concepts which are less directly related to children's experiences, are more difficult to experience through the senses, drama or other vicarious experiences and are more difficult to define than specific concepts.

At **Level III** are the **key concepts** with their high level of abstraction, broad scope and openness to differing meanings and interpretation. These overarching key concepts are capable of being used to further illuminate and enrich an individual's understanding of the subordinate and specific concepts from the lower levels. The model assumes that the learning of concepts for children of primary age is most often likely to proceed from the specific to the general. Teachers, in both planning and in teaching, are assumed, as adults, to be able to move amongst the three levels.

The HGSS Project provided materials for use in schools which were intended to be guidance and support for teachers and to illustrate ways in which themes could be structured to encourage the development of skills such as the ability to evaluate information and the exercising of empathy and to develop children's conceptual understanding. One Unit, *Rivers in Flood* (Schools Council, 1976) used geography alone as its resource; others, *People on the Move* (Schools Council, 1976) and *Life in the Thirties* (Schools Council, 1976), used the combined resources of geography, history and the social sciences. In all these materials, the project's main purpose was to present authentic resource material from the social subjects for use with young children. Examples could be chosen from any of these materials but the focus will be on *Rivers in Flood.*

Rivers in Flood
This Unit was designed for children in the 9–11 age range, with potential for use not only at Key Stage 2 but also at Key Stage 3. It is not possible to produce the actual materials in the text and therefore it is impossible to do them justice.

Rivers in Flood addressed three questions:
1 What causes floods?
2 What is their effect?
3 How do people adjust to the flood hazard?
As a too often occurring natural hazard, the threat of flood is a condition with which many communities have to learn to live. The costs in life and property is staggering. For example, a Mississippi flood in 1974 was estimated to cost 80 million dollars. In 1993 the flooding of the Mississippi is estimated to have cost 2 billion dollars. Some parts of the world live with the inevitability of floods. Bangladesh is described as 'that geographical coffin of the thousand rivers.' *Rivers in Flood* as a Unit had to make sense to teachers and children the nature of living with floods.

Schools Council Projects had no power to direct or to prescribe, they could only influence and persuade. The HGSS Project was a complex innovation and was perhaps before its time in the 1970s because at that time objectives were not general currency with teachers and the notion of key concepts was far too distant from most teachers' thinking.

In addition, a middle years project could be dismissed by both primary and secondary teachers as being irrelevant to them and projects which named two or three subject areas together could often be interpreted as another integrated studies project. Marketing the idea of the HGSS Project was therefore difficult.

To be successful, innovations needed to be legitimated by influential individuals or groups in order to bring them onto the planning agenda of busy teachers. Local Inspectors and Advisers and HMI were recognised legitimators. In general, the History Inspectorate supported the project, the social sciences lacked HMI support and the geography Inspectorate remained agnostic about the project. The geography Inspectorate welcomed the use of objectives but remained unconvinced about key concepts. Bennetts developed objectives for teaching geography quite separately from the project and quite clearly had an influence on the DES document, *Geography from 5 to 16* (DES, 1986). Other official publications in the late 1970s and early 1980s had significant affects on the fortune of the HGSS Project. The Primary Survey of 1978 and the Middle Schools Surveys of 1983 and 1985, in their different ways, influenced views that teachers had or were developing of the project (DES, 1978, 1983 and 1985). The 1978 Report saw the social subjects in primary schools as 'random and repetitive', in that much of the work under this area of the curriculum consisted of unplanned or opportunistic topics on themes which were repeated year by year.

The Middle Schools Reports of 1983 and 1985 criticised unsystematic approaches to geography in particular and the social subjects in general. Geography in the middle schools was said to lack a conceptual basis with pupils having no knowledge of the concept of location or spatial awareness in their thinking. Teachers were seen to be lacking in skills and knowledge of a geographical nature. Their initial and in-service education needed changes to cope with these gaps in their knowledge and practice.

Although the HGSS Project had addressed all these issues and had emphasised the need for a framework for curricular planning, by the early 1980s the influence and impact of the Schools Council had faded away. The concerns of the time were falling rolls, lack of resources and an increasing call for accountability as both the development of appraisal and the prospects of a more centrally directed curriculum appeared on the horizon.

The discussion document in the HMI Series on *Geography from 5 to 16* (DES, 1986) covered much of the same ground as the HGSS Project. The suggested structure for progression and continuity from lower to upper primary into secondary education emphasised many of the same approaches. The objectives for the teaching of geography contained in this document echoed those advocated by the Schools Council Project. According to the HMI discussion document, children in later primary years were to be encouraged to acquire skills in the following areas:

(a) carrying out observations and collecting, organising and retrieving information as part of an enquiry;
(b) using a variety of sources of information;
(c) communicating their findings and ideas, with varying degrees of precision, in writing, pictures, models, diagrams and maps. (p.12)

In addition the development of appropriate language and mathematical skills related to their geographical education. Equally important, geography was to be used as a resource through which children learned to:

'appreciate the significance of people's attitudes and values in the context of particular environmental or social issues which they have investigated'. (DES, 1986)

From the above quotations the correlation with the objectives of the HGSS Project are clear. Thus by 1986, the date of publication of the HMI geography document, the development of values and attitudes were still central to the teaching of primary school geography.

The HMI document did not advocate this use of key concepts but found a more effective way than that of its Schools Council predecessor. Primary children, according to the HMI, were to study the **local area, unfamiliar places, location and spatial relationships.** They were also to develop map skills and **the skills of geographical enquiry.** Each of these areas was followed by a set of key questions to be addressed by teachers with children, and also included objectives to be followed. For example, some of the questions related to the development of location and spatial relationships were framed on the notion of **place** and were:

— Where is it located?
— Why has it been located here?
— What movements occur between these places?
— What are the routes linking these places, etc?

It is not the purpose of this chapter to deal in any detail with the contents of the National Curriculum for Geography. It is hoped that a picture of an approach to the curriculum for geography for the primary school has emerged from the work of the HGSS during the 1970s and later work by the HMI during the 1980s. Although differing in emphasis, there was essentially a consensus in this work. The Schools Council Project could in no way be prescriptive and the work of the HMI became increasingly so, not in detail but in laying down frameworks for primary geography and relating content and skills to levels and to suggested sequencing of content and advising on what progression in learning might be for young children learning geography.

The innovations of the 1970s and the 1980s attempted to take away the randomness and repetitive nature of much primary geography while maintaining the integrity of the subject. The National Curriculum, in contrast with what went before, is prescriptive in terms of content, framework and notions of levels of learning and conceptualisation appropriate for each of the Key Stages and Levels.

In attempting to encourage the development of values and attitudes into young children's geographical education, the work leading to the National Curriculum attempted to provide a curriculum which helped teachers and children together to explore the values and attitudes of individuals and groups in relation to these issues.

Tackling sensitive issues with young children, although being demonstrated as being fruitful in the work of the HGSS Project and later work, met with resistance in the 1970s and was often and is still misunderstood by many teachers. Dealing with sensitive issues with young children is itself a sensitive (and political) issue. In addition, values and attitudes are difficult if not impossible to assess. As we moved towards a National Curriculum which is assessment-led, value issues were taken out of the programmes of study. There is also another opportunity being lost for providing children with the experiences of investigating value issues related to their own lives, the environment and to global issues. Geography, as a resource, is not being used to its full potential for this purpose. Countering this argument by claiming that such issues are best handled in Cross-Curricular Themes such as Environmental Education, Economic and Industrial Understanding and Multicultural Education, is shunting value education into a siding where the ideas are marginalised. When assessment is supremely important, those activities that are not assessed are clearly given a low priority. The primary school geography curriculum remains, in this sense, 'risk free', which is where the team of the HGSS Project found it in 1971.

CHAPTER 3

Making a Place for Geography: The Geographical Association's Initiatives and the Geography Working Group's Experience

Wendy Morgan

Geography, that stimulating subject which encourages the inquisitive nature of young children, helps them to understand their immediate environment and opens doors to a wider world, has not had a very high profile in primary schooling in the recent past. Now, with geography securely placed as a foundation subject in the National Curriculum for England and Wales, its subject matter clearly defined and with the Geographical Association supporting primary teachers' efforts to implement it, the subject seems to be facing a much more propitious future.

The Geographical Association: pre-national Curriculum

Prior to the introduction of the National Curriculum the Geographical Association had very few members in the primary sector. A sample of 3,400 personal members subscribing to *Geography* or *Teaching Geography* in 1986 yielded only 78 teaching in junior or middle schools, whereas 1,790 were secondary school teachers.

From at least the 1960s onwards, the Primary Schools Section Committee was in existence, later responding to school reorganisation post-Plowden to become the Primary and Middle Schools Section Committee. This small group met termly and was more or less synonymous with the Section, in that only one or two additional members appeared at the annual general meeting, who were immediately enrolled as committee members.

Nevertheless, from the 1960s onwards, four editions of a primary geography handbook were published by the Geographical Association, increasing in size and complexity with each edition. The current publication, edited by Mills (1988), is the all-time best seller among the Association's publications, having sold around 10,000 copies. A successor to this handbook is being written – specifically to help teachers with National Curriculum geography, while promoting general good practice in the event of changes to the Order for geography. The occasional article in *Teaching Geography* and a special focus section in June 1987, a few small publications, and a section newsletter, was, until recently, the extent of primary publishing by the Geographical Association.

A primary contribution, often a symposium, became a regular feature at the annual conference from the late seventies onwards. This was planned and led by members of the Committee and attracted good attendance from advisory staff, and secondary as well as primary teachers. During the build-up to the National Curriculum a national primary conference was held at Leicester in July 1986 to consider the role of geography in the education of 5–11 year olds. An excellent attendance made this probably the first major conference on primary geography held in this country.

The Geographical Association's role in establishing geography in the National Curriculum has been described elsewhere (Bailey, 1991). Provision for the subject at primary level, both in the National Curriculum and within the Association itself has always been problematic. From 1987, when it became clear that, as a foundation subject, geography would be taught in primary schools, the Association made major moves to support its development. From May 1989, when the Geography Working Group began making plans for the Attainment Targets and Programmes of Study which would be the basis of National Curriculum geography, the form of the primary content and its relationship to geography taught by specialists in the secondary sector were fiercely debated. These two strands will be considered in tandem in this chapter.

Primary Geographer established

In 1988, when it was clear that geography would be a statutory requirement in all primary schools and for all pupils aged 5–11, the Geographical Association set up a sub-committee of Council to consider the implications for the Geographical Association. The sub-committee proposed a special category of membership for primary teachers and schools, with a magazine to support it. Council and the annual general meeting approved the proposal and in due course *Primary Geographer* was established alongside *Geography* and *Teaching Geography.*

The new magazine was made available termly on subscription to individual subscribers or to corporate bodies, mainly primary schools. The subscription rate, unlike that for the other journals, was the same for both categories. Subscribers became full members of the Association (a fact not always understood even now), which enabled them to buy publications at reduced rates and enter fully into Association activities. The first issue appeared in March 1989 and was mailed free of charge to every primary and middle school in the U.K. This costly undertaking did not at first seem to have been very successful, as many teachers claimed not to have seen it. As there is no reason to think that the mailing went astray, it is likely that copies simply went missing in schools, where large quantities of unsolicited material frequently appear in the post.

In due course subscriptions began to be paid and the first issue in October 1989 went out to 1,000 subscribing members, the majority of whom were primary school teachers. From then on enthusiasm for the magazine was considerable. The autumn term 1989 saw the formal requirement that geography should be taught in all primary schools. Teachers unused to teaching geography found the magazine a boon. Any early criticisms that the content was too difficult were silenced when the Geography Working Group's reports foretold the demands which the National Curriculum for geography might make of both pupils and teachers.

The magazine was originally issued for a trial period of three years, its continuation dependent on meeting a target of 3,000 subscribers in that time. Although there was some uncertainty about the timing of the three year period, whether from March or October 1989, in the event the figure was exceeded by a very comfortable margin and the magazine continued to thrive. Now, after four years, the number of subscribers has passed 5,400 – doubling the Geographical Association's membership, which rose to well over 10,000 in its centenary year of 1993.

Primary Geographer has been remarkably fortunate in its contributors. No writer has ever refused to give material for the magazine and all the prominent experts in primary geography have contributed. Regular series as well as one-off articles alternate with project materials and reviews of books, materials and software. Full page colour photographs provide a useful resource, as well as providing messages about the nature of primary geography for generalist teachers.

Subject matter covered in the early issues considered the nature of primary geography and suggestions for work in the classroom and out of doors. As the content of National Curriculum geography was revealed, articles became more sharply focused, increasingly addressing the needs of teachers as these were expressed at INSET sessions and courses. Advisory staff and teacher trainers not only contribute articles, but also promote the magazine while using it in their courses. Two LEA advisers bought subscriptions for all their primary schools for an introductory period of one year. As teacher expertise increases it is hoped that more teachers will be confident enough to contribute articles about their own implementation of geography.

Primary subscribers have also received, since Autumn 1991, a free copy of the Association's newsletter, *GA News*. This contains a column devoted to primary concerns, as well as news of vital concern to all teachers of geography. Since October 1992, *Primary Geographer* has increased in size from 16 to 24 pages and is now published not three but four times each year. This has allowed some space for advertising, which provides an additional service to teachers, while offsetting some production costs. In October 1994 expansion to 36 pages is planned.

The Geography Working Group

Clearly the success of the Geographical Association's primary ventures was affirmed by another successful initiative – its political lobbying in the mid-1980s, ensuring a statutory place for geography in the National Curriculum. The appearance of Bailey and Binns (1987) *A Case for Geography*, finally convinced Kenneth Baker, then Secretary of State for Education, that geography should be given the status of a foundation subject in the National Curriculum. This ensured that it would have to be taught to all pupils from the age of five.

After much speculation about its leadership and personnel the Geography Working Group was set up by Kenneth Baker in May 1989 to advise him on the Attainment Targets and Programmes of Study appropriate for the subject. Members were chosen as individuals, not as representatives of any group. Nevertheless eight of the thirteen were actually Geographical Association members, including three past or future Presidents. Sir Leslie Fielding, a career diplomat and Vice-Chancellor of Sussex University, was appointed to chair the group. A year was allowed for deliberation, during which nearly twenty meetings took place, some of which were residential over two or three days. A final report was to be made in April 1990, with an interim report in October 1989. The Group received no pay (expenses were reimbursed), but those in full time employment found considerable difficulty in integrating the work of the Group with their own professional responsibilities, let alone family commitments. Confidentiality was imposed so no consultation was possible beyond the Group once work began, a feature which disadvantaged me as a generalist among specialists.

During the previous year the Association set up its own shadow 'Geography Working Group' to help prepare members for the negotiation and consultation which would be a feature of the development of National Curriculum geography. Three of the chosen members of the official group had also been associated with the Association's group. The publication resulting from this shadow group's work, *Geography in the National Curriculum* (1989), edited by Daugherty, was published just before the formal Geography Working Group was appointed. It contained tentative suggestions about Attainment Targets, Programmes of Study and content. I was able to hand Mrs Angela Rumbold, then Minister of State for Education, a copy of the book at my interview for membership of the Group. Later the book was made available to all Group members for our consideration.

I soon found that I alone among the members of the Group had taught in primary schools. Nor was there a lecturer experienced in the training of primary teachers. Only one member, an LEA adviser (a second was appointed later), claimed knowledge of the primary phase. The HMI assessor was also familiar with primary as well as secondary schools. Not only was I the only primary practitioner, and the only generalist educator without specialist training in geography, I was the only member who had taught the whole curriculum – a fact which was to prove equally significant. Inability to confer with colleagues outside the Group increased my sense of isolation and my burden of responsibility for the first two Key Stages.

Attempts to create a primary focus within the Geography Working Group

Early in the Geography Working Group's programme, members were given an opportunity to offer to colleagues a personal view of geography. In the first instance this was through the selection of a significant chapter or article which was circulated for all to read. Unable to locate a piece of geographical writing which adequately presented geography with a primary flavour, I offered my colleagues a selection from Sybil Marshall's book about her village primary school in Cambridgeshire (1963). The extracts demonstrated how a teacher faced with pupils aged 5–11 in one class, tackled personal studies of far away places, map interpretation, landscape and weather studies, local surveys, contours and creative work based on the local environment. All these were closely integrated into topics and projects arising from the children's needs and interests. The effect on the Group cannot be gauged, but one member admitted to visiting the village where Sybil Marshall worked as a result of enjoying the extracts. Subsequent readings of the extracts to teacher groups led to a meeting with one of the 'children' concerned and eventually to a meeting with Sybil Marshall herself. Her astonishment that I had selected geographical extracts when geography was her 'worst subject' was equalled by her enthusiasm for the National Curriculum which she believes will restore rigour to the primary curriculum.

Secondly members were invited to present a tentative proposal for the shape of the curriculum in terms of Attainment Targets. Prior to this I had circulated known primary geographers for their views on content and with this in mind developed a model in three dimensions and bright colours to present my view of geography. In effect it presented strands of physical and human geography as ATs, with expanding scales (places) in a different dimension, and skills as an implicit background with environment and world citizenship at the heart. However the contributions of my weightier colleagues were given more attention and my efforts to provide a vivid demonstration of the nature of geography as it pertained to younger children may well have been regarded as peripheral.

A framework for the geography curriculum

The selection of a suitable model on which the curriculum could be based formed the main agenda of early meetings. The rival appeal of models in which place and enquiry were major components was debated. Lack of experience in curriculum development and an embargo on seeking advice beyond the Group left me unable to make a firm commitment to either point of view. My main concern was that the structure chosen should not jeopardise the firsthand, active, enquiring geography which should characterise primary practice. Nor should it encourage large numbers of case studies which would dilute quality geography by overloading the curriculum.

Eventually a model was chosen, at an extra meeting inserted during August, when the four members most closely associated with schools were on pre-booked holidays and therefore absent from the Group. Five of the nine ATs proposed were devoted to place. My worst fears were realised as colleagues proposed a proliferation of case studies and lists of locations to learn as suitable fare for the primary sector. At least 44% of the proposed content was concerned with distant places. My suggestion that 15% at Key Stage 1 and 20% at Key Stage 2 was a more appropriate proportion was rejected out of hand by the chair.

During the meetings that followed, my attempts to regain a balanced programme for primary geography were submerged under the varied concerns of other members, speaking from a background of secondary and HE geography. My position within the group became increasingly isolated and beleaguered. At length an additional member, an LEA Adviser, was appointed ostensibly to 'strengthen primary representation'. I suspected that he was brought in to weaken my opposition and to confuse my message. My confidence was further undermined by a reprimand concerning the History Working Group. My attempt to contact the two primary members of that Group led to concern among the civil servants and a meeting of the two chairs. Although my intention was merely to gain support and advice about how to keep primary concerns afloat in the Group, I was accused of breaking confidentiality and usurping the chair's role of communication with the other Group.

After several meetings in which my views were never seriously considered I decided on more vigorous intervention. A paper delivered verbally to the whole Group in October expressed my gravest misgivings about the emerging geography for Key Stages 1 and 2. The Group heard me out in silence, but the chair immediately called for a break in the meeting, after which discussion of my concerns was reduced to a minimum.

Publication of the Interim Report

The resulting Interim Report (the ATs were by now reduced to eight of which four were devoted to place) offered to the Secretary of State and to public scrutiny (though not official consultation) proposed that primary pupils should learn 155 items of locational knowledge and carry out eleven separate case studies of places in the U.K. and around the world. At their most bizarre these included a major world city study, an island study (choice of five in each case), a National Park and a major industrial region in the U.K., as well as a study of population growth in California.

Before the fury of teachers was unleashed on the Working Group I wrote my own condemnation of the proposals in a strongly worded paper which spelled out in detail my objections, while distancing myself from the proposals. My concluding paragraph was as follows:

'Our proposals for Key Stages 1 and 2 in the Interim Report do not add up to a coherent, child-related curriculum which stands any chance of being delivered satisfactorily by generalist teachers to ordinary children. In seeking to be politically and academically respectable we have designed a structure which is inappropriate at this level. In attempting to apply geography to the TGAT model through this structure we have failed to achieve a coherent policy for Key Stages 1 and 2, and have not even sought to identify such policy within currently recognised good practice. The HMI report, *Aspects of Primary Education: The Teaching and Learning of History and Geography* (1989) clarifies features of good practice and gives cases of well structured activities, successfully carried out. We have ignored their implications, building an edifice which is educationally indefensible, dealing a crushing blow to those teachers who eagerly await sure foundations on which to build geography in the primary school.'

I was clear at this point that unless radical changes took place I could not support the Geography Working Group through to the end. However if I resigned, there was no other primary practitioner or generalist teacher to defend Key Stages 1 and 2 against inappropriate proposals.

The public response

The unofficial consultation brought forth a flood of responses in a wide variety of forms and expressing a multitude of often conflicting views. The proposed method of analysis could not cope with the volume and diversity, so members read as many submissions as possible and commended to others those they found most significant. Only a small proportion of respondents commented on the primary proposals, all of which I read. Sadly their views were so inconclusive that they gave me little help in arguing my case. At least, once the proposals were made public, discussion with primary colleagues was possible again and my confidence became somewhat restored.

In a further attempt to show Group colleagues the enormity of the content for primary pupils I designed a series of topic proposals which drew in all the Statements of Attainment for both Key Stages. The links between SoAs were tenuous, but by means of a large number of topics delivery was possible. Misunderstood again, my attempt was dismissed as irrelevant because I had used the teachers' discredited device, the topic web, to demonstrate links between SoAs. A subsequent exercise on overload had colleagues from higher education and industry assessing the content of Key Stage 1 geography and judging its suitability for $7^{1}/_{2}$ per cent of curriculum time.

Responses were still pouring in as the Group continued the second phase of its work. Although there was never an admission from any member that our original plans were badly awry, significant changes began to occur as Attainment Targets were reduced to seven, Statements of Attainment were rejected and rephrased and attempts to create coherent Programmes of Study were made. Ideas, wordings and objections were logged prior to the final drafting, and made the responsibility of one member. Throughout this period the views of huge numbers of geographers and geography educators continued to flow in. Frequently dismissing these as vested interests, some members displayed uncharacteristic arrogance in the face of so much criticism. My continuing opposition to major areas in the proposals were seen by some fellow Group members as obstructive as the deadline for the Final Report approached.

Preparation of the Final Report

When the draft of the Final Report was presented to the Group it was clear that a major shift in emphasis had taken place. The primary proposals were much more suitable and were considerably reduced in extent. In the ensuing discussion I was reticent about suggesting further changes for fear of losing the ground already won. In the rewriting our representative had achieved a miracle of diplomacy which removed 90 per cent of my objections. Perhaps my interventions had had some effect after all! The major problem still remaining was the increase in complexity from Level 4–5. Time ran out as we attempted to adjust content across the Levels and the Key Stages and found ourselves unable to do more than reiterate SoAs in the Programmes of Study. Deliberately the latter were designed to cover only average Levels, that is 1–2 for Key Stage 1 and 3–4 for Key Stage 2. Examples were added to each SoA in the last few days. The Final Report was delivered on time at the end of April, completing the work of the Geography Working Group.

Consultation and the Order for Geography

Formal consultation then took place, with a committee set up within the National Curriculum Council to note responses and adjust the proposals accordingly. Their report duly appeared, reducing the ATs to five, with place now slimmed to one AT but given triple weighting for assessment purposes. Other adjustments to SoAs played havoc with the integrity and coherence of the original proposals, though others lightened the load for primary teachers. The alarming conceptual threshold between Levels 4 and 5 remained, a hazard for able young geographers in the primary school. Finally, before the proposals became law, a Draft Order was published. This marked the arrival of Kenneth Clarke as Secretary of State. Kenneth Baker set up the Geography Working Group; John

McGregor received its reports. Kenneth Clarke took a knife to the proposals, hacking out controversial issues and aspects of enquiry. In the uproar that followed, few realised that he had inadvertently benefited primary geography by removing some cumbersome and unsuitable material – particularly at Levels 4 and 5. Though the step from 4 to 5 remains steep, it is now less hazardous than previously. The Order for geography was finally published at Easter 1990, prior to the start of implementation in the following Autumn Term.

In spite of all the problems associated with its design, a statutory curriculum for geography was now in place. For the first time, geographical education was an entitlement for every child throughout the primary years. A major task lay ahead in supporting teachers through the early stages of implementation, but the statutory nature of Attainment Targets, Programmes of Study and assessment procedures ensured that primary geography could no longer be ignored.

The Geographical Association and the Geography Working Group

Throughout the development of National Curriculum geography, the Geographical Association lost no opportunity in trying to influence the outcome. The book prepared by the Association's National Curriculum Sub-committee was part of the preliminary reading of the Geography Working Group. Further submissions concerning geography's links with other subjects and cross-curricular elements were made. At one meeting a delegation of four Association officers met with the members of the Group for a short period, during which the visitors were permitted to make statements but no discussion was allowed. A detailed and substantially critical response to the Interim Report represented the views of 2,000 members derived from well-attended regional meetings. Following another round of regional meetings, a response to the Final Report submitted to the NCC sought to rewrite the Programmes of Study. Throughout the whole exercise the Association did its utmost to represent its members' often very critical views.

Support for primary teachers

Once it was established that geography would be a statutory part of the primary curriculum, the Geographical Association lost no time in seeking to support its rapidly growing primary membership. *Primary Geographer* provided the initial means of support, and readers have testified to the success of the magazine in this respect. Immediately after the publication of the Order for geography the Association responded with a stream of support booklets for teachers on a range of topics related to KS1 and 2. A total of twenty or more publications have been produced in the first two years of National Curriculum implementation, which are relevant and useful for primary teachers. They include two photo packs featuring distant localities, initially one of the hardest parts of the new curriculum to resource. More titles and photo packs are in preparation.

Primary provision at the annual conference of the Association has been greatly extended. From the modest beginnings of a single lecture or seminar grew the now well-established Primary Day. This has become traditionally the opening day of the conference, occurring in London in 1988, 1989 and 1990, and then moving with the conference to Manchester in 1991, Southampton in 1992 and to Sheffield for the Centenary conference in 1993. Large numbers of primary teachers from all over the country have thus been able to take part in this free event, whether members of the Association or not. Attendance on Primary Day is usually around 500, and recently many more primary delegates have been resident for at least part of the conference. Increasingly other parts of the conference also offer matters of interest to those concerned with the education of younger children. It is to be hoped that a national conference mounted by the Primary and Middle Schools Section in October 1993 will also become an annual event and move round the country providing INSET opportunities while attracting new members. The current initiative which aims to coordinate INSET on a regional basis has been largely motivated by concern for the primary sector. It is likely to result in additional conference provision for primary teachers. Another initiative called the Primary INSET Package offered a day's INSET provided by three Geographical Association primary experts to an LEA or a group of schools. Perhaps because the price was too high, or because the publicity was minimal, this has only been mounted on two occasions. The first diploma course validated by the Association was completed in mid-1991. Taught as a 'twilight' INSET course at a Teachers' Centre and staffed by a college of HE, it is hoped that this will be the precedent for many such courses. Five of the successful teachers were primary generalists.

The annual Geographical Association Award for materials to assist the teaching of geography at all levels, has never received so many entries prior to the publication of the Order for geography. Entries include book and non-book materials, both published and unpublished. The materials for primary schools have been significant in quantity, coverage of both Key Stages and in the diversity of resources submitted. In 1992 one of the first publications designed to support geography in infant classes was awarded the Gold Award in competition with entries for all phases of education.

During the development of the National Curriculum for geography one of the oft-repeated objections to aspects of the curriculum related to the lack of suitable resources. This was particularly so in the matter of localities overseas, those in developing countries being regarded as most problematic. The response of publishers was immediate and specific. In only a few months new and imaginative approaches to resourcing the curriculum and supporting teachers emerged. Aid agencies and other charities including the Geographical Association provided resources focusing on localities overseas, particularly in developing countries. A photo pack featuring Choglamsa Tibetan children's village in Ladakh, northern India was produced by members of the Geography INSET Primary Project Steering Group at the University of Liverpool and published by the Geographical Association. Packs featuring aerial photographs, a wide range of atlases, course books for both Key Stages, topic books, wall-charts, maps, teachers' books and globes have all been published in direct response to the new curriculum.

The Geographical Association has sought to establish links with other bodies interested in promoting primary geography. The links with the Geography INSET Primary Project have probably been the most fruitful. The Associate Director of the GIPP is a co-opted member of the Primary and Middle Schools Section Committee. She also serves on the Editorial Advisory Panel for *Primary Geographer.* The honorary editor of *Primary Geographer* in turn serves on the GIPP Steering Group. The Director of GIPP is a member of the Geographical Association Council in company with three other members of the GIPP Steering Group. Yet another member serves on the Association's Education Standing Committee. These links have led to the exchange of views and ideas related to the development of geography in the schools and particularly to the identification of areas of greatest need for teachers implementing the subject from a low knowledge base. (The Association was represented on the committee of the Primary History Association, until its merger with the Historical Association.)

The Geographical Association is gradually changing the focus of its constituent standing committees, section committees, working groups and working parties to embrace the interests and needs of non-specialist teachers who are now teaching geography. Several of these groups have now acquired at least token primary representation, and this will increase in due course. New groups are currently emerging with a brief which includes major primary components. The President for 1992–3, the Centenary Year of the Association, was an ex-primary teacher, the first to reach such high office. Additionally the sixty-five branches of the Geographical Association, covering most of the country, many of which have traditionally catered for sixth form interests, are now seeking to attract primary teachers to their meetings.

Underpinning all this recent activity, the Primary and Middle Schools Section Committee coordinates all primary initiatives within the Association and attempts on a very limited budget to provide services for its primary members. This is now a very different role from that undertaken only a few years previously. This small group can take much of the credit for turning the Association into one of the few subject associations which is really addressing the needs of its primary teacher members.

Towards a philosophy for primary geography

National Curriculum Geography is not yet in its final form. It is to be hoped that the review by Sir Ron Dearing, set up by Secretary of State John Patten, will mould the current Order into a more acceptable form for the primary sector. It is to be hoped that Programmes of Study will emerge which are specific to each Key Stage and which replace much of the Level 5 material in Key Stage 3 where it rightly belongs. An adjustment which removes much of the burden of assessment, while retaining detailed guidance about the nature of geography, would also be welcomed. The opportunity for teachers to choose from non-statutory parts of the Programmes of Study while the core remains statutory also seems a positive proposal. Studies of local and non-local localities could form a useful core.

In spite of all the activity surrounding primary geography in recent months, one important deficiency remains. The National Curriculum has not yet provided us with a philosophy for primary geography. Many of the Working Group's critics claimed that the Final Report was watered down secondary geography and that the curriculum derived from it is not matched to the best primary practice.

It is to be hoped that the final outcome of the Dearing Review will provide a framework for geography which is specific to the Key Stage for which it is intended and compatible with pupils' level of development. For each Key Stage the balance between geography which can be taught through fieldwork, particularly in the local area, and that which demands secondary resources, should be appropriate. The balance between the essential core of the subject and the optional non-core should be enabling and not restrictive. Places and themes to be studied should be as broadly outlined as at present and maximum use should be made of developments in curriculum planning, INSET and resource provision.

The emerging philosophy for the subject should embrace infants finding their way around the school, nine year olds swapping letters and photographs with classes in the next town, and eleven year olds using E Mail and FAX to communicate with fellow Europeans. It must facilitate fieldwork on the school site, in the locality, on day trips and residentials. It must cover home-made weather instruments, and tray models and play mats, as well as Ordnance Survey maps, aerial photographs and satellite imagery. It should encourage thoughtful youngsters and teachers who question the world around them to seek to make it a place fit to live in now and in the future.

The philosophy for geography in the primary school will not be created by government Order, nor by the publishers of textbooks and resources. It will be created by teachers and children, working with the support of projects such as GIPP and subject associations such as the Geographical Association, who reveal the heart of the subject and justify its inclusion in the education of every primary child.

PART B

Implementation

CHAPTER 4

New Thinking in Mapping

Jim Martland

Introduction

There appears to be a commonly held view that young children have difficulty in understanding, reading and using maps. Recent research with young children, aged 3–6 years, has shown, however, that they can possess the concept of a map and how it can be used (Freundschuh, 1990; Spencer et al., 1989; Ottosson 1988). Intrigued by these findings, I began to reassess my approach to the teaching of mapping skills. I had long been aware that the skills portrayed in primary geography texts were not necessarily those required when a child used a map to make a journey or tackled fieldwork.

In this chapter I set out how I created a teaching programme for mapping skills which draws heavily on firsthand experience and discovery. In conducting the teaching with over 400 children aged between 7 and 11 years I discovered that orientation of the map and the ability to update one's location on the map as a route is followed are key skills. This account charts the pedagogical journey I made, and its subsequent implications for the teaching of primary mapping skills.

The Purpose of the Mapping Programme

Stage 1: Exploration and Discovery

In designing the programme of mapping skills, I began by reflecting on how the first explorers and navigators had performed. Finding out what exists in a new area is compelling, exciting and potentially hazardous, but we all possess a desire to make sense of the world we are in. Having discovered what exists, we have a need to communicate this both to ourselves and others either verbally, pictorially or symbolically, as we may wish to revisit the area or describe to others how to get there.

The overall aim of my programme was to equip children to understand what a map is and how it can represent information. I wanted the children to be able to draw maps which they would use to set and solve problems which involved navigation.

For the initial exploration an area is selected such as the classroom, hall or a small part of the school grounds, and a set of objects set out to create a landscape which is novel to the child. These can be natural objects, play equipment, or school furniture. Thus while the general area may be very familiar, and therefore provide security for the young explorer, the actual terrain which is presented is new. The area I used for my teaching was the central courtyard of an infants' school which possessed flower tubs, sand and water areas, benches and items of play equipment. A number of small coloured objects such as discs, skittles, or cones were set out on or near to the major features. The first task was to explore and to discover that these features exist. In the beginning this can take the form of free exploration but incentives can be given for the children to look carefully in all parts of the landscape. For example, you can ask the explorers to find five yellow cones, three blue skittles, or to touch certain features. Such challenges add purpose and encourage searching movements throughout the terrain.

Moving about the area can also be encouraged by asking each child to select and stand by one of the minor features, say a cone, and then visually work out a route to another cone. On the signal the children move to different positions. In this exercise all the children move. However, you could ask one child to move and touch each of the other participants.

As confidence grows in moving about the area so does speed. To encourage moving quickly to different destinations and to work out routes under pressure, a game called 'Remove One' was devised. Each child stands at one of the coloured cones and they have to move to a new cone on the signal. However, one cone is removed. Since only one child can be at each location, one will be 'homeless'. The game is repeated until only one child remains.

Initially, I had set out the location of the objects which had to be found. Now I wanted the children to decide where objects should be placed. Since these had to be clearly visible we constructed streamers cut from multi-coloured plastic which were attached to clothes pegs. Each streamer was given a code letter and the whole was stored on a card. (Figure 4.1)

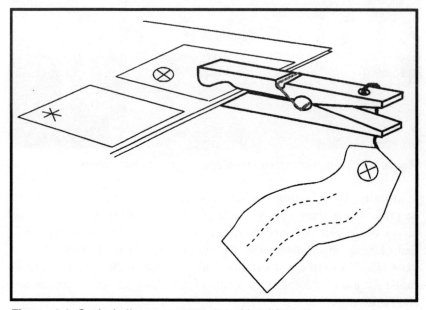

Figure 4.1: Coded clip on streamer and baseboard

The children were asked to select their own location and attach the marker. Games, similar to the ones described previously, were repeated using the children's positions. (Figure 4.2) This activity lends itself to practising the language of spatial relationships. Telling others where objects are and how to get to them is a natural consequence of the identification of a location.

The position of each streamer in the terrain possesses three relational, descriptive attributes which I refer to as the triad of spatial information. First, the streamer is placed on a feature which has a name; second, the streamer is a certain distance from other features; and third, it is in a specific direction from other objects. The location can always be named, though the direction and distance is more complex as they may be specified in relation to the position of the giver of the information, the recipient or indeed other features.

Figure 4.2: The children run to place or collect streamers

Initially, the children tended only to use duos of information to describe where their streamer was placed. For example, 'It is on the corner of the plant tub over to my right' – (feature and direction specified). Later, longer statements were generated which combined 'it's in front of', 'it's beside', 'it's in line with', or 'it's in the centre of', indicating the use of the spatial concepts of proximity, direction, succession and enclosure.

We played 'What is the feature?' – a game where the children had to describe the location of the streamer without actually naming the position. This activity led to the formation of longer sentences such as 'My streamer is on a feature which is between the sand pit and the door over to my right and it is near to the blue table.' The advantage of this exercise is that one person can describe the location but everyone can try to solve the problem. No movement is necessary.

The directional instructions become more complex when we have to describe to another person how they can reach the location of the streamer. For example, 'From where you are, go to the blue table on your right. Then turn to face the sand pit. Go past the sand pit until you come to the bench near the plant tub and then go forward three paces to the blue cone.' It is difficult to comprehend and recall such a list of commands. Just think how we as adults have to repeat and check directional information when we are asking how to get to a destination. The children thought out their instructions and then gave them one sentence at a time as their partner completed each stage of the task. With experience the children could give and receive series of instructions.

To make the language more overt and also to place the emphasis on listening to instructions, one partner was blindfolded and taken to a new starting point. The person giving the directional instructions walked behind trying to give clear, accurate information in order that the 'blind' person could reach the location. The children enjoyed this activity and even challenged the blind person to retrace the route they had taken without wearing the blindfold.

Stage 2: Making the Map – the Need for a Permanent Record

The activities of exploration and discovery, the specification of locations, route generation and route execution had been conducted without the need for a map. Now the children were presented with a problem. I asked, 'How would you describe to others what your newly discovered world looks like?' 'How could you keep a record of your discoveries and journeys so that you could repeat them?' They suggested remembering and telling others, drawing pictures and making maps. Each idea was evaluated. You will notice that the word 'map' came from the pupils.

The drawing of a two-dimensional representation of the features and locations which they had selected is a very demanding task. In anticipation of events, I provided a large rectangular sheet of card which mirrored the shape of the courtyard.

I set the card in the same orientation as the area and positioned the children behind and around me so that they could view the terrain from my perspective. The card was placed horizontally and we discussed the important features on the boundaries of the area which they thought should be included. This is an important step in map-making as the accurate depiction of boundary features provides the frame of reference for the siting of features. The earlier exercises, which had focused on the triads of spatial language, were most helpful now in deciding specific locations. The children undertook a most important consideration in map-making – that of deciding which objects should be included. Having located the point on the 'map', they discussed how to represent the feature. Shape is obviously an important consideration but colour is also meaningful at this stage. I encouraged the children to describe how we should draw the feature. I was not concerned at this point whether they suggest plan view, elevations or pictorial images – rather that they understood which feature the image represented and that it was in the correct spatial relationship to other features on the boundaries of the area.

The boundary information was copied on additional sheets and the children, working in small groups, began to map the features they wanted to include. The group had to agree the location of features on

Figure 4.3: Discussing and drawing the map

the map and take turns in drawing (see Figure 4.3). The drawing of the map and the discussion of the locations and symbolism proved to be a

Figure 4.4: A 'map' of the area: the spatial relationships are correct

revealing practical assessment task. At this point I did not want to insist on 'correct' symbolism, nor to compare how other groups had represented the area. The map was their representation. They created it and had ownership of it. Now they were going to use it to make new journeys and discoveries. Any discrepancies, key omissions, and errors would be revealed, and perhaps amended in the process of using the map. Finally we discussed the value of giving the map a title and date. We also felt that it was important to add the names of the map-makers. They were proud of their maps and I photocopied them so everyone could now become a map user by being both a problem setter and solver. (Figure 4.4.)

Stage 3: Planning and Following Routes

The possession of a map presented the opportunity for a wide range of activities. I split each group into pairs. The children had the task of surveying a route around the terrain and drawing it on both maps in red pen. I introduced two new symbols, the triangle symbol for start and a double circle for finish. Each pair gave one of their maps to another duo who had to use the map to follow the route. The problem posers meanwhile tracked the progress on their master copy and gave the navigators feedback on how they had tackled the journey. (See Figure 4.5.) It can be seen in the photograph that the problem posers have their pen or fingers on the exact location of the solvers, each group is reading and using the map. The pairs continued to exchange maps and follow the

Figure 4.5: Planning and drawing a route-following problem

routes. The task was extended by making more complicated routes which involved crossovers and the children chose the additional symbolism of arrows to show direction.

Additional extension activities can be created by walking the reverse route. Since both the navigator and the problem setter have maps, I posed the question 'How could you help someone who you notice is beginning to make a mistake when following your route?' We decided that the problem setters would shadow the wayfinders and tell them immediately they made an error. This soon developed into the shadower walking one metre behind, not speaking, but tapping the wayfinder twice on the shoulder if a mistake was made, effectively saying, 'Think again!'

The Problems of Map Contact and Orientation

When you use a map to follow a route, two novel problems emerge which are not present in book-based exercises. The first concerns knowing where you are on the map at any given moment and the second involves keeping the map orientated.

The problem of keeping track of progress along the route was solved by the process of 'thumbing the map'. The map is held in both hands but the index finger, or thumb, is used to follow one's position along the route, constantly updating the information as features are passed. The children, following the progress of others on their map, had discovered this technique but failed to use it in their own wayfinding. It is a simple but effective skill which builds confidence. We practised keeping contact with the map, using more complex route-following exercises in different environments. On the command 'stop', each child had to place his or her finger on their exact location.

Orientation, however, presents a more complex problem. By orientation I refer to the ability to keep the map in correspondence with the features on the ground so that what is on the left in the terrain will be shown on the left of the map and vice versa. Similarly, features in front of you will be 'at the top of', or 'away from you', on the map. I shall continue to use the word 'orientate' though many adults use terms such as 'to put the map the right way round', 'to set the map', 'to align' or 'line up the map'.

Orientation errors appear when wayfinding because the natural behaviour of the map user is to retain a constant grip on the map. This is appropriate when travelling forwards with the map orientated. However, problems occur when changes of direction are made. The grip is not relaxed and so the map continues to be held orientated to the map reader and not the landscape. Adults acquire skills in reversing the images mentally and so can continue to effect a correspondence, but mental reversal is a complex task for the beginning map reader. Failure to maintain orientation and contact with the map leads to errors in wayfinding which may lead to becoming lost. Negative experiences of this kind lower confidence and enjoyment and can colour attitudes to future map work.

The ability to maintain orientation is vital in wayfinding, but how can it be taught? I decided to begin by asking 'What does a person need to know, understand and be able to do, in order to orientate a map?'

Let us assume that you know where you are in the landscape and that you can identify your current location on the map. The map can be orientated to the terrain by matching information from the terrain and relating it to the map. Say, for example, we could see a large linear feature, such as a wall. This can be located on the map and the map turned so that the wall is parallel to the information on the map. Similarly, we can identify point features and align them with the symbols. Other features may also be identified and checked so that what is on the left in the world is on the left on the map. Whether one starts from features in the landscape, or symbols on the map, the process of orientation by landmarks requires multiple sets of information.

Clearly an experienced map reader will not have difficulty in achieving this, but is this method applicable and appropriate for a seven year old? Is there an easier way?

My experiences of using map and compass in the sport of orienteering indicated that there was. If the magnetic north indication on the map is matched with compass north, then a map can always, in any circumstances, be orientated. More importantly, this learning only requires one set of information which can be summed-up as 'Map North to Compass North'. I decided to pursue this line of thinking but first I had to overcome two obstacles. First, there was no simple compass on the market, reliable and accurate enough for the purpose and, second, north on maps tended to be shown by one small, conventional symbol.

I submitted a design to Silva Compasses (UK) Ltd, and they agreed to supply prototypes. The Model 7DNS compass (Figure 4.6) has a large, clear compass housing in which the red, north-pointing needle settles quickly. The first problem having been overcome, I now had a tool to work with. I overcame the second problem by superimposing on the maps several red, north-pointing meridian lines. These culminated in red arrows and so compass orientation for young children could be reduced to matching a red needle to a red arrow or 'Red to Red'. Accurate orientation of the map can be achieved by positioning the

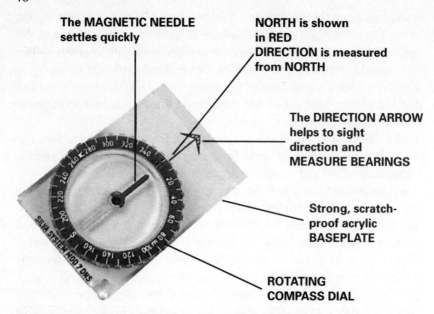

The **MAGNETIC NEEDLE** settles quickly

NORTH is shown in RED DIRECTION is measured from NORTH

The **DIRECTION ARROW** helps to sight direction and **MEASURE BEARINGS**

Strong, scratch-proof acrylic **BASEPLATE**

ROTATING COMPASS DIAL

Figure 4.6: The Silva Direct Compass Model 7DNS

magnetic compass needle along a meridian line and turning the map so that map north matches magnetic north. This task, whilst simple in concept, is difficult manipulatively for children as both the map and compass are held as one unit. Placing the map on the ground is helpful, but I prefer a slightly less accurate method of orientation which is easier

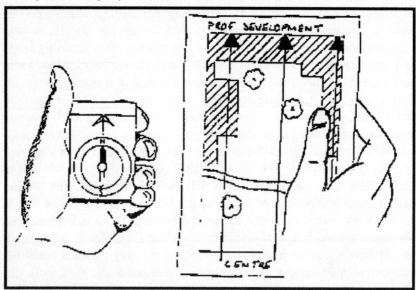

Figure 4.7: Orientating the map with a compass

to handle. Here the compass is held in one hand and the map in the other. The compass is positioned parallel to the meridian lines and the wayfinder turns until the red magnetic needle points in the same direction as the red meridian arrows. This method is shown in Figure 4.7.

I now wished to establish in a more scientific way whether young children could solve orientation problems on a route-following task. Space does not permit a full report (but see Martland and Walsh, 1993), but the following gives sufficient indication of the scope of the research.

A sample of 83 children from four Year 3 intact classes was selected. All were given a simple familiarisation activity, Test A, which required them to use a pre-marked map to traverse a route across a grid of squares, 40 feet by 40 feet. The starting point on the map was indicated by a red triangle, and the junctions through which the route crossed were identified by a red, numbered circle which corresponded with a numbered disc in a container on the actual grid. Test A together with Test B are shown on Figure 4.8.

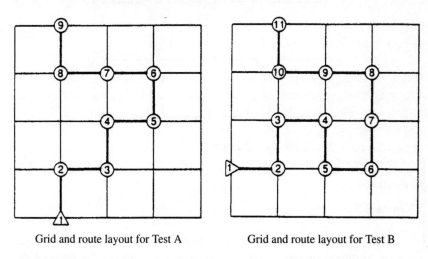

Grid and route layout for Test A   Grid and route layout for Test B

Figure 4.8

All the children completed Test A with little difficulty. A second test, Test B, followed. This presented a route which had combinations of turns requiring movement through 180 degrees, thus heightening the probability for disorientation. The number of errors made and the time taken indicated that Test B was more difficult. In fact 73 per cent of the children made orientation errors.

It was now necessary to intervene by giving the children specific orientation strategies. One class received instruction on orientation by landmarks, the second orientation by compass, the third received both landmark and compass orientation, with the fourth class acting as a control. Each class received four lessons of instruction and were then tested. Test C again involved a wayfinding task across the grid. Landmark information was shown by an array of coloured cones. The map to be used showed both cones and magnetic north meridian lines in red. (See Figure 4.9.)

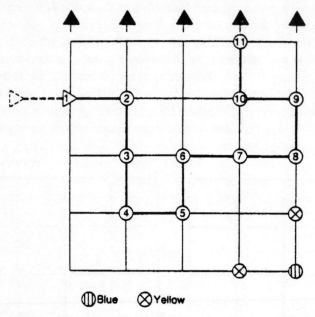

⦀Blue ⊗Yellow

Grid and route layout for Test C showing magnetic north information and landmark information.

Figure 4.9

Each child was offered the map and a compass and therefore had access to either strategy to solve the problem. The results showed that there was a statistically significant improvement in the children's ability to maintain orientation for those who had received the tuition. More importantly, 62 per cent of the children who had been given both compass and landscape strategies chose to use the compass to maintain orientation.

Conclusion

The investigation into my teaching began by a consideration of research which indicated that children as young as three to six years of age were capable of working with maps. I investigated a novel approach to map-making and map use for wayfinding which involved exploration and communication. In the process of this study I became aware that the skills of orientation and map contact were necessary if children were to use maps accurately and with confidence in a fieldwork setting. My subsequent research revealed that children aged seven could orientate maps with the aid of a simplified compass and that this method had preference over orientation by landmarks, the reason being that only one set of information is required for this task, i.e. matching map North to compass North.

The implications for teaching are clear. Children's large-scale maps should possess several north-pointing meridian lines terminating in a red arrow. Indistinct, single black arrows are not useful. Secondly, the map should be used in conjunction with a compass. I would also suggest that orientation is such an important concept and skill that children should be taught to ensure that every time they stop on a journey they should orientate the map, that they should not set off along a route until the map is orientated, and finally that when the map is orientated to the terrain the landscape and map can be read directly ahead. Mental reversals are not necessary. The whole can be summed-up under the caption: 'Correct orientation with good map reading is safe wayfinding.'

It can be claimed that this pedagogical journey has not been just an academic one. To follow up the research, Silva Compasses (UK) Ltd have now marketed the Model 7DNS compass together with a handbook of guidance for teachers. (See Martland and Walsh, 1993b)

CHAPTER 5

Resourcing Primary Geography: Bringing the World into the Classroom

Jo Hughes and Bill Marsden

Background

A resource, in its dictionary definition, is a means of supplying some want or deficiency: a stock or reserve which can be drawn upon as necessary. Geography is a strongly *resource-based* subject. It uses resources common to other subjects, and some which are more distinctive to geography. As in other subjects, a narrow range of resources will have a narrowing effect. If geography was no more than a factual recall subject, all the resources needed would be the teacher, chalk and talk and an information type textbook, with verbal information and perhaps a few maps. Clearly a subject taught in this way would have virtually no justification for a place in a forward-looking curriculum.

A rich harvest of resources is central to fulfilling the aims of geography, as an enquiry-based subject, as presented in earlier chapters. The most obvious resource for good practice in geographical education is the environment as directly experienced. In general, primary teachers are adept at acquiring the necessary range of resources for their own local patch, and the onset of the National Curriculum has widened the awareness of the range of resources that is available, and sharpened insights about those which are distinctive to geography and those which help also to cross the boundaries between disciplines. Thus the map, while most distinctive to geography, is also a vital resource for history, and can also profitably be deployed in developing skills in language and mathematics.

The focus of this chapter is not on the resources required for direct study in the local locality, but rather on those that are necessary to 'bring the world into the classroom' in the investigating of distant places. The ideal is to find, for places which must be explored indirectly, as rich a range of resources as can be collected for the home area, so simulating or even recreating an equally vivid environmental experience.

Rather than providing checklists of materials that can be used for such a study, we are going to describe how we went about acquiring the materials for a distant place locality study. This was one which could function as an overseas locality study: in this case, as an overseas locality for Key Stage 1, or as a means of permeating the European dimension with themes for Key Stage 2. This chapter therefore links with the final chapter in this book, in which the context of a broader European dimension is considered. In this chapter, therefore, we will concentrate on the distinctively geographical element, though at the same time not neglecting the cross-curricular possibilities.

The initiative we describe arose from our Geography INSET Primary Project (GIPP), one of the tasks of which was to provide distance learning materials for primary schools. In this case, we were approached by a local headteacher, who had received a grant from the Central Bureau for European Exchanges, to help him to develop a European locality study. How would this be resourced and how would we go about it? Obviously the key point was to experience the area we were to select for investigation, which meant finding more resources. One of us also obtained a Central Bureau grant, and the other received some support from the Project. The first resource of geography we regarded, almost as an article of faith, as that gained 'through the soles of the feet', *through preliminary fieldwork*. Though it may not be practical to take a whole class of children abroad, a distant place study obviously gains if the teacher has had firsthand experience of it.

Our first task was to decide on the locality to be chosen. We gave priority to a study in Spain, specifically related to the Barcelona region. One reason was that Barcelona was topical as an Olympic City, and always has been and will continue to be a European city of outstanding importance and interest. Another reason was that one of us had contacts in Barcelona. In the end we found the cheapest way to travel was to take a package holiday in late-September to the Costa Brava region, with the intention of covering localities not only in Barcelona, but also in Catalonia, including a small Costa Brava resort. The resort we chose was Blanes.

Resourcing a European Locality Study of Blanes

Why select Blanes?

Ideally one of us would have previously spent time in Blanes and become aware of its geographical potential. None of us had been to this area and the choice had to be made on second-hand, but still revealing information. One reason we selected Blanes, at the southern end of the Costa Brava, was because it was accessible and the only resort on the Costa Brava coast on the railway to Barcelona, which we wanted to visit as well (Figure 5.1). Perhaps the clinching reason was that we found in the Baedeker Guide an oblique photograph taken from a hill overlooking the resort which suggested it was a small town with high potential for geographical study. Figure 5.2 is a black and white version of this photograph. From this and other information in easily obtained brochures and guides, we found before we travelled that Blanes:

(a) was, as already mentioned, a coastal resort;
(b) was a small fishing port;
(c) had its own central shopping area and a weekly market;
(d) had a botanical garden of international significance;
(e) was located in the midst of some spectacular coastal 'capes and bays' scenery.

Criteria for choosing resources

Before going to the trouble of seeking out the range of resources we knew we would need, it was important to decide the criteria on which we should choose those resources. There are three broad groups of criteria we have always found useful for this and other types of evaluation in curriculum planning in geography: will the resources support good practice in –

(a) geography;
(b) primary pedagogy;
(c) social education.

It is clear that the tourist materials obtainable from a travel agent fail on these grounds, useful though they in some ways are as resources. They are characteristically dedicated to offering a simplified and exotic view of a place, enhancing differences rather than similarities, and promoting stereotypes rather than a balanced portrayal. While they might contain material of geographical interest, this is not their purpose and the geographical content is limited. Thus they might offer climatic detail which tells us how much sunnier the climate of the Costa Brava is than, say, that of London. For geographical education purposes we need

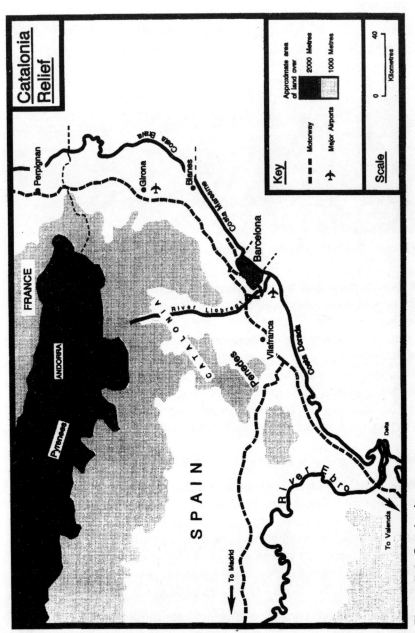

Figure 5.1: Catalonia map

Figure 5.2: Photographic panorama of Blanes

a fuller picture. And while they present material of potential interest to primary children, they need much supplementation to fulfil the criteria we have indicated.

It was important for us, therefore, as teachers, to find the resources which would give us a more balanced, up-to-date and authentically geographical understanding of the Costa Brava in general, and of Blanes in particular. Consultation of various books and articles offered us the following geographical résumé. Note that this résumé was put together as a resource for the teacher, rather than for the children.

The Geography of a Tourist Area as a Resource

Relief. Catalonia includes the eastern end of the Pyrenees and its associated foothills. These are made up of a variety of rocks and have produced very irregular and *dissected* country over the region, with narrow *coastal plains* in some areas, and an *indented coast* of *bays and headlands* (capes) in others. (Figure 5.1) The Costa Brava, the 'wild coast', (see Figure 5.1), contains both spectacular cliff scenery and extensive sandy beaches, as in the area of Blanes.

Climate. Catalonia has a *Mediterranean-type* climate, with autumns and winters that are mild and wet and summers that are very warm and dry. It is, however, distinctly different from the much warmer winters and the very hot summers of the Costa del Sol. These are in general more congenial for British visitors than the Costa Brava in winter, but less so in summer

From the teaching point of view, it is useful to look at similarities and differences between the climate of a distant place and that of one closer to home. Thus Barcelona's average temperature for the year is 15.2C as against 9.8 for London. Rainfall for Barcelona is 538mm. per annum as compared with 605mm. for London. October temperatures average over 16.0C, while the rainfall in that month is higher on average than in south-east England. It should be borne in mind, also, that while the amount of rainfall is not vastly greater in London, it falls in Britain on a lot more days, while Catalonia tends to receive more of its rain in heavy downpours, especially in summer and autumn. This greater number of sunny days is clearly a great advantage from the point of view of the tourist, and it is this aspect that is seized upon by the travel agents. In creating an authentic picture of the geographical environment, it is important not to stereotype an area as being bright and sunny all the time, when this is not the case.

Tourism in the Costa Brava: economic and environmental aspects. Tourism has formed an important element in the Spanish economy since the 1950s, not least in Catalonia. It provides about 10 per cent of the GNP of Catalonia. The province has about 20 per cent of Spain's hotels and 40 per cent of non-hotel accommodation in apartments, guest houses, and on camping grounds. Much of this accommodation is related to the trend in Spain for second homes, particularly concentrated in the Barcelona metropolitan area, with advantages such as access to the sea, and a burgeoning growth of marinas.

In the last thirty years tourism has been especially helped by

(a) the ending of the Franco regime in 1976;
(b) entry to the EC in 1986;
(c) improved communications from the late 1960s, including, in the case of the Costa Brava, the opening of Gerona as an international tourist airport and a motorway connection between the French frontier and Barcelona (A–17);
(d) upgrading of the local railway north from Barcelona which links the resorts of the Costa Maresme, but leaves the coast at Blanes.

Environmentally the Costa Brava has not suffered from unchecked coastal development as greatly as southern areas such as the Costa Blanca and the Costa del Sol. While the massive sprawls of resorts like Benidorm and Torremolinos have largely been avoided, the impact of urban development on the Costa Brava has, however, been considerable. In particular, the presence of many small local administrative units has made overall planning difficult. A good deal of the tourist development is of a shoddy quality.

Resources for a Study of Blanes. Blanes, a small town of nearly 20,000 people, is still too big as a whole to be counted as a genuine locality study. It offers various possibilities for a number of different locality studies, however, and a lot of potential for *permeating geographical skills and themes,* including:

   (a) the harbour area (fishing port and marina); and
   (b) the central area covering the resort and shopping area.

It illustrates very well the different *strands* of the National Curriculum in geography, and offers many opportunities for relating those of physical, human and environmental geography. It is vital, not least in time benefit terms, to make optimal use of these opportunities.

Relating Physical and Human Geography. As with agriculture, the study of the tourist industry effectively links physical and human geography including the following geographical *strands:*

• Weather and climate and economic activities (tourism)
• Landforms (coastal) and settlement.

The Coastal Landforms. The resource material here is particularly coloured photographs which we took but which cannot be reproduced in this book for cost reasons. The photographs have been fully used in our courses with teachers and could equally be for work with children. The following landform concepts are illustrated:

• An *indented coast* made up of alternate *bays* (sandy) and *headlands or promontories* (rocky cliffs);
• *Marine erosion* producing *cliffs and stacks* (stacks are isolated pillars or blocks of rocks which were once part of a cliffed headland, cut off from the main cliff line by wave erosion concentrated along steeply inclined joints);
• *Marine transport and deposition* carrying material and depositing in *bays,* as in the case of Blanes, where there are good examples of *bayhead beaches;*
• Blanes also has the unusual feature of a *tombolo* formed by deposition of sand to form a *spit* which links a small island to the mainland.

Effects on human geography.

1 The indented coast includes sheltered bays, and the leeward side of these bays can be used, as at Blanes, for harbours for fishing boats and, increasingly, as marinas for pleasure craft (Figure 5.2).

2 The low-lying land behind the bay is frequently built up in a settlement which, with the growth of the tourist industry, has expanded onto the hills behind.

3 On the promontories, as at Blanes, high quality modern housing can be found, overlooking spectacular coastal scenery.

The Fishing Industry of Blanes. Blanes comes tenth among the fishing ports of Catalonia. Catalonian fishing is, however, on a relatively small scale as compared with that of north-west Spain, where long-distance trawlers are based. The fishing fleets of Catalonia mostly concentrate on local coastal waters and on serving a local market. The *advantages for fishing* include:

(a) Mediterranean fishing grounds offshore;
(b) the sheltered harbours of the indented Catalan coast, such as Blanes;
(c) the importance of fishing in the traditional local diet, producing a continuing basic demand;
(d) the nineteenth century growth of large cities such as Barcelona, greatly increasing the demand;
(e) the more recent growth of the tourist industry, increasing the demand for fish products in hotels and restaurants.

Going to Blanes. The preliminary work on providing the geographical background resource, crucial though it was, left much still to do. Continuing the need to pursue good geographical and good primary education practice, it was necessary to focus down on the common need to acquire resources that *promoted enquiry-based learning.* This meant using firsthand resources and finding other resources that help to answer enquiry-type questions, of the now familiar type, which include:

— Where is the place?
— How do we get there?
— What is it like?
— Why is it like it is?
— How is it changing?
— What must it feel like to live there?

All these need to be resourced. To answer the first question we obviously require a range of maps. To answer the second we need access to travel information, such as route maps and timetables. To answer the third we need in particular a range of photographs, collected on the visit. To answer the fourth and fifth questions we need the type of material we had also already collected, and is part of the resource background offered above. To answer the final question we again critically needed the actual experience of being in the place. As already noted, the

58

essence of bringing the particular distant place into the classroom is access to a wide range of resources.

There follows a list of resources we collected mainly on our visit. Unfortunately we can only describe them here. Remember the majority of them were in colour.

1 A wide range of *maps* is always necessary and was provided here. For an overseas locality study there are problems of finding original Ordnance Survey-type materials. For this there are two possible sources. One is an important map shop like Edward Stanford in London. Another is the Spanish equivalent of one of our Ordnance

BLANES: Central Area

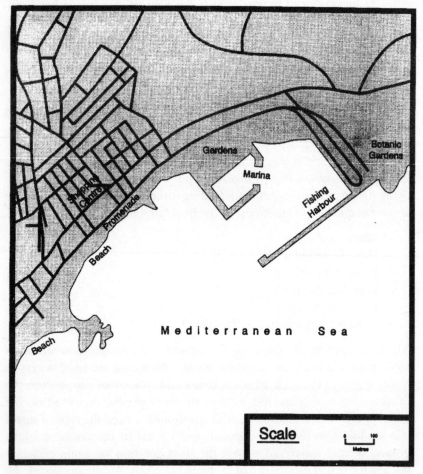

Figure 5.3

Survey agencies, in this case in Barcelona. From these we were able to obtain, for example, a 1:25 000 scale map of Blanes. From the tourist office in Blanes we obtained a straightforward street plan, from which we made our own simplified map (Figure 5.3).

2 To say that taking a range of *photographs* is equally as important as acquiring maps is almost restating the obvious. They are particularly important at primary level because less abstract than maps. The photographs collected included:

    (a) a vertical aerial view of part of Blanes, obtained from the Spanish Ordnance Survey office in Barcelona;

    (b) a very large selection of photographs in slide or print form taken from vantage points (see Figure 5.2);

    (c) postcards of scenes we could not have taken ourselves (for example, historical photographs on postcards).

Different sorts of visual resource are needed for Key Stage 1 and Key Stage 2 purposes. Thus for Key Stage 1, it is important to take relatively simple ground level photographs of scenes that can be related to familiar ones of the home environment, such as street furniture, shops, street markets, signs, and individual buildings. It is also vital at this stage that the photographs should include people, not least with the children of distant places, often engaged in similar activities to those followed at home.

3 A lesser, so far as geography is concerned, but still important element in developing skills of graphicacy is the ability to draw and interpret *graphs,* which links in well with National Curriculum Programmes of Study in mathematics. For Key Stage 2 at least, this can be associated with sets of climatic figures both for, in this case, the Costa Brava, and also the home area.

4 *Diagrams,* which can of course be of many types but which here include a three-dimensional relief model of the Blanes area, obtained from the Spanish Ordnance Survey, as background to the work on physical geography.

5 *Timetables,* for example, air timetables, illustrating connections between England and Gerona (or Barcelona), and rail, illustrating connections between Barcelona and Blanes, need generally to be simplified by the teacher, but offer many opportunities for enquiry-based work, like, how long does it take to get betwen places?, where do you have to change?, and so on.

6 *Second-hand textual materials,* already referred to, which include:

(a) easily accessible and free tourist brochures for the Costa Brava;

(b) also easily accessible purchased tourist guides to Catalonia (Michelin, Baedeker, etc.);

(c) travel books, often available in cut price book stores;

(d) textbooks and academic articles on the geography, history and culture of the area;

(e) materials collected in Catalonia in the original language.

7 *Memorabilia,* collected, like photographs, with the intention of evoking a 'sense of place' in the classroom – what is it like to live there? One problem is to try to avoid too much of the exotic souvenir type of material. Good examples for geography include:

(a) bus and rail tickets;

(b) guides to museums, botanic gardens, castles, etc.;

(c) menus (frequently in different languages on the Costa Brava);

(d) local newspapers in the indigenous language (relevant extracts);

(e) package labels of familiar products in the local language;

(f) adverts (photographs of or taken from local newspapers, etc.);

(g) posters and stickers, characteristic of the local area;

(h) local postage stamps (note that stamps, apart from maps and photographs, are the most geographical of all resources);

(i) T- and sweat-shirts, etc., with local connotations;

(j) local currency (and currency tables), credit card transactions, etc.;

(k) weather forecast maps and tables (in local newspaper);

(l) plans, e.g. of Barcelona airport;

(m) local TV and radio programme details (in local newspaper);

(n) flags and other recognisable 'patriotic' items.

Summary

This analysis of how we set about finding resources for a study of a distant place, in our case, Blanes, thus highlights key elements in resource collection in geography.

• In the first place, *geography itself must be seen as a basic resource,* providing relevant and up-to-date detail, tied into recognised conceptual frameworks which are essential aids to curriculum planning and serve to avoid problems of superficiality and stereotyping (see also Chapter 2).

• The most authentic resources for geographical study are different types of maps and different types of photographs.

• Creative resource collection is an integral part of the curriculum planning process, and not merely a preliminary to it.

• The resources you collect yourself, like the photographs you take, have most meaning for you and usually will provide the best teaching material.

• You do need, however, to develop basic skills of landscape photography, use a decent camera and good quality film, and aim for something more geographical and of better quality photographically than conventional holiday snaps.

• Going to a place yourself is of great importance. Your own geography is best learned, as we have already said, through the soles of the feet. Try to find ways of resourcing visits for contrasting locality studies in Britain and Europe. Remember that some of the cheap holiday breaks, if you undertake them out of term time, are no more expensive and maybe less so than having supply cover during term time. Clearly going abroad for such purposes is not always possible, in which case using friends or relatives abroad, or having twinning arrangements with European schools (see Chapter 12), may be a viable alternative. Obviously it is also useful to supplement resources you have collected yourself by the purchase of the now plentiful 'locality packs' and geography schemes which include locality studies of areas you would be unlikely to be able to visit yourself.

CHAPTER 6

Curriculum Planning in Action

Ashley Kent

Introduction

The intention of this chapter is to portray, in detail, how two schools are putting into operation the geography National Curriculum. It is hoped that these portrayals will offer insights for others engaged in primary geography. Further case studies at both individual school and LEA levels are also worth studying in Naish (1992), particularly as they portray the early process of teachers responding to the geography National Curiculum.

In the case of this chapter the schools were chosen for a variety of reasons. Firstly they were recommended to the writer by advisers/inspectors of their respective LEAs; secondly they were different types of schools in different parts of the country; thirdly they drew children from a range of backgrounds.

The writer visited both geography co-ordinators at their schools and subsequently invited them to modify his versions of their conversations. As readers can see, there is a set order of reporting on the schools, starting with general observations about the school and ending with the geography co-ordinator's views on the geography National Curriculum.

School One

St Mary's Church of England Primary School is in Colton (population 780), a village outside Rugeley in south Staffordshire. It has 63 children aged 4 to 11, though it could take up to 93. Most pupils live in the village but 25 per cent or so come from Rugeley and its surrounding area. Generations of local families have attended the school. This is now very much commuter land since it takes about an hour to get to Birmingham and twenty minutes to Stafford. The pupils come from a variety of social backgrounds but the majority are professional. When the children get to nine some are lost to the middle school system, particulary to Alleyne's School, Uttoxeter, or to Oldfields Middle School then on to Alleyne's High School at 13.

Staff. There are 2.7 staff! Reception and Year 1 are taught in the mornings by the part-time member of staff and in the afternoon by Lyn Evans, the headteacher, and Wendy Horden the other full-time teacher. Years 2 and 3 are taught by Lyn and Years 4, 5 and 6 by Wendy. They lost a third full-time member of staff in April 1993 because of budget cuts.

Geography Co-ordinator. Because of the small size of the school, Wendy Horden is not only curriculum co-ordinator for geography but for science, IT, PE and history as well. The co-ordination of the entire National Curriculum has to be undertaken by the two full-time and one part-time member of staff. Wendy is also the geography cluster co-ordinator for the three schools in the primary school 'cluster' in this part of Staffordshire – St Mary's is one of these three schools. She went to Matlock College of Education where geography was her main subject, with PE her minor speciality. She has taught six years in a middle school as a general class teacher, then four years as a head of department in a similar school. She worked four years part-time in a local small school and at the same time was part-time advisory teacher for geography. She has been full-time in her present post for one year.

The Geography Curriculum. As early as March 1992 Wendy had helped to establish a geography policy for the 'Rugeley Small Schools Cluster'. This has naturally influenced the St Mary's curriculum. Part of the curriculum plans she has developed are shown in Figures 6.1 and 6.2. Linkages, progression and revisiting are clearly important working principles as these curriculum plans indicate. A particularly important curriculum resource developed by the school is its conservation area. This consists of an embankment, pond and wildflower garden adjoining a stream. There are trees and nesting boxes and children are encouraged to walk through the area throughout the year.

Teaching Strategies. Because classes are all of mixed ages they are split into ability groups for most of the time. Class teaching is difficult but does occur with differentiation by task, catering for different abilities and age groups. The staff consequently have to be very well organised and have to rely on children making considerable use of the library (and in the case of geography, atlases). This, of necessity, means that independent learning is standard for these children.

Visits. They recently have established a school twinning with a Walsall school where 80 per cent of the children are Bangladeshi and recently took a coachload of children there, intending to visit every two years. They also have established links with a school in New Zealand and an estate school in Lichfield. The latter came through Wendy's membership of a 20-day Geography GEST course and is intended to provide data for a contrasting locality study. They also regularly visit Shugborough, its farm, house and museum. They use an outdoor education centre in Chasewater, undertake urban work in Lichfield and visit the two other schools in the Rugeley cluster of primary schools.

The quality of the work St Mary's does in its own locality has been recognised by Staffordshire LEA and as a result Wendy and her children were filmed by a TV film crew in June 1993 as they undertook their locality studies. There is to be a series of five programmes on Channel 4, the first broadcast in Spring 1994, entitled *Geography Starts Here*, in which St Mary's locality study forms one of the three case studies.

Resources. There is support for this cluster in the form of the help of the Staffordshire inspector in charge of small schools. The cluster pools resources and this year there has been an extra £200 for history and geography. The school does not use textbooks but a variety of other resources. They have acquired a good number of maps of their locality at a range of scales. They have also bought a good range of one-off atlases and have purchased an aerial photograph of the school and its vicinity which they plan to use as the basis for calendars! Through the LEA geography adviser and GEONEX they are to purchase a pack of 15 aerial photographs of their county to go alongside the set of 36 or so photographs taken by their own pupils of their immediate locality.

Wendy has purchased globes for each classroom though they need to purchase world maps in wall-map form for Class 1 and Class 2. The cluster is building up a library of videos recorded off air by Wendy on behalf of the group. She does not regard herself as particularly computer minded but does use databases and wordprocessing (CAXTON and WRITE software). In addition, the school has a Nimbus micro in each classroom as well as two 480Zs in addition to two Nimbuses which circulate around the cluster. They use LOGO particularly to draw maps of Colton. There is to be 'pyramid' support from an advisory teacher to help the school incorporate IT within the curriculum (from September 1993 onwards). They also find local newspapers a useful resource, particularly for finding out about places and current issues.

Training. Wendy started in June 1993 a 20-day DfE GEST geography course, part of the work of the North West Consortium of Staffordshire, Shropshire, Cheshire, Lancashire and Cumbria. The course was co-ordinated by the GIP project at Liverpool University's Department of Education. An integral part of the course was a planned fieldwork visit to Barcelona which will generate materials on the European dimension in geography (see Chapter 5).

Views On National Curriculum. Wendy personally does not have problems with the geography National Curriculum but feels it does not give enough guidance to non-geographers. She feels much has been left out and that the links between geography and science are not overtly made, though teachers are discovering these for themselves. It gives teachers a great deal of work but she considers the development good because it encourages 'focused curriculum planning based on a subject'. However, she does feel that the geography Order is too vague for the non-specialist, and that schools are in danger of teaching to the ATs and forgetting the value of PoS. She dislikes the lack of standardisation of levels across subjects and worries that teachers will teach just to the document. Time, she considers, is the big problem and pupils are feeling that they are moving on too quickly from topic to topic. On the other hand when some of her pupils took pilot SATs, she was amazed at how much they knew!

School Two

Beaconside Infants School is in Penrith, Cumbria, and has a roll of 190 children aged four to seven. There are reception classes and classes for both Years 1 and 2. The intake varies slightly each year, so for instance in 1992/93 there were 58 children in two reception classes whereas in September 1993 there were 75 children in three reception classes. The school with its adjoining junior school is in eastern Penrith, the most rapidly expanding part of the town. Its catchment consists of a wide range of housing types, much of it new housing and consequently there is a wide socio-economic mix of intake. The school has a high proportion of pupils with special educational needs. There are eight full-time teachers in addition to others, particularly those who help pupils with special needs. There is, as the headteacher puts it, 'reasonable' staff stability. Three responsibility allowances are available and these vary year by year according to priorities indentified by the school development plan. Last year (1992/93) the priorities were home/school liaison; maths; and appraisal. This year (1993/94) they are IT and PE. Pairs of teachers work together on the planning of subject areas so in the case of geography the co-ordinator works with a new teacher in her third year of teaching and they together are responsible for planning the subject.

Geography Co-ordinator. The geography co-ordinator at Beaconside is Stephanie Fearn who is also the headteacher. Geography was Stephanie's main subject at college – Keswick Hall, Norwich. She undertook a primary science course run jointly by St Martin's College, Lancaster, and Cumbria LEA in 1981 and became an advisory teacher for primary science in north Cumbria. For fifteen years she has been on the committee of the Cumbrian Association for Environmental Education, fully involved in its activities and publications. The other half of the team, Katherine Dredge, will take an increasing responsibility for geography as she gains more experience.

The Geography Curriculum. Before an LEA inspection in March 1993 the staff were unsure as to how much geography *per se* they were undertaking. The subsequent report (Figure 6.3) suggested they were successfully completing a good deal of geography. They feel little pressure from the National Curriculum in their planning of work for the reception classes but Years 1 and 2 are planned together as a whole curriculum, structured round topics. At the beginning of Year 1 they plan in detail for Year 1 and more in outline for Year 2, aiming to achieve balance and breadth over the two years. They work carefully at PoS and ATs and make sure they are 'covered' over the two year block. Subjects are considered within the topics.

Teaching Strategies. The school has an open plan design and this enables team teaching through topics. As Stephanie suggests, 'topics' is a 'dirty word but we shall carry on'. The staff tend to plan the work then consider the appropriate teaching strategy and a wide range of the latter are used. 'You name it, we do it', remarked Stephanie. They use a wide range of ability groupings in the school.

Visits. In reception there is a good deal of use of Penrith and the immediate vicinity of the school. They work in the school grounds and the streets around the school. They visit the town station, castle, shops, cattle market, watch houses being built, cranes in operation and drains being relaid. This all complements the houses topic for the summer term last year. When possible they try and visit Carlisle or other local towns by train or bus during the better weather.

In Year 1 the trips vary according to topic planning but frequent visits are made around and about Penrith to study old and new shops for instance. At least two trips are made outside Penrith during the year by coach to a woollen or water mill; or to Carlisle Castle; or to Wethriggs

Pottery. A particular highlight this year has been a visit to the Lake District with a focus on the study of farming. Figures 6.4 and 6.5 outline the Lake District topic.

In Year 2 after Christmas there is often an 'out of county trip'. In 1993 they visited Beamish, and Bradford in 1992. In the case of the latter they compared Bradford town centre with Penrith and visited the National Museum of Photography. On the topic of 'journeys', in Year 2 they take a ride on the Settle–Carlisle railway.

Resources. The school is about to buy a set of 10 aerial photographs (vertical and oblique) of important sites throughout the county, through the good offices of the LEA geography adviser. This also includes a photograph of the school. The set has cost £80 or so. The big inflatable globes they have bought have proved extremely useful, especially the physical geography ones. They have also purchased several picture packs of physical features, orienteering equipment, and a big collection of wall-maps of the British Isles and the World. They have marked the playground with a compass and a library collection of textbooks is being established. Class sets of textbooks have not been bought and they tend not to use printed worksheets. They do use videoed TV programmes intended for adult audiences but without the sound track. Computers are used for data handling to do with journeys and travel agents, distances of journeys and types of weather in different resorts. They have purchased a wide range of atlases designed for infants and particularly like the pictorial atlases now published. They make their own wind measurers (speed and direction) and use giant three feet high thermometers with the addition of their own scale from cold to hot.

Training. After an INSET day on geography in early 1992 they developed 'Towards a geography policy' (Figure 6.6); similarly after another staff meeting in March 1993 they took account of the suggestions discussed (Figure 6.7).

Views on the National Curriculum. Stephanie likes the geography AT1 but dislikes AT2, seeing it as singularly inappropriate for infants in the way it is phrased. She does not see why AT2 cannot be spread across the other ATs. She likes physical geography (AT3) but has difficulty in intepreting its SoAs. It is 'nonsense for the non-specialist teacher – needs to be more specific'. She would like to see the geography Order more like art and music where there is an end of Key Stage statement with very specific exemplars of what pupils should be able to do and understand. In other words, clearly defined steps *en route* are, she feels, needed to help non-specialist teachers. Stephanie finds environmental geography very difficult for infants whom she argues are unable to express likes and dislikes. Their reasons are often very superficial. She does not want assessment to be withdrawn from foundation subjects otherwise they would be devalued. She has had the opportunity to express these views since the Dearing Review has called on her to attend regional and national conferences.

Final obervations

There were various common elements in these two case studies. In the first instance it is clear that these are two well-established, well thought of and oversubscribed schools. Their geography co-ordinators are active, involved and influential beyond their own school gates and both had specialised in geography at college. Both have been advisory teachers, have a wider range of other responsibilities beyond geography and are actively co-operating with their own and other primary staff. The geography curriculum in both cases is driven by and has resulted from meetings leading to policy statements. A wide range of teaching strategies and fieldwork/visits programmes are common to both. Each has adopted an eclectic approach to the purchase of resources and consequently each has a wide range. Both co-ordinators broadly welcome the geography National Curriculum but are sceptical as to its value for non-specialist teachers, feeling it ought to be more specific.

Overall this writer could not fail to be impressed by the energy, flexibility, expertise, openness and positive approach of these teachers at a time of unprecedented change and pressures on staff. With no doubt similar commitment and professionalism being displayed by teachers across the country, the future of geography education for primary pupils looks rosier than it has done for some time. The immediate challenge for government and schools is to ensure that the majority of primary school teachers delivering the geography National Curriculum are trained up to the task such that they develop the expertise and enthusiasm of a Wendy or a Stephanie!

69

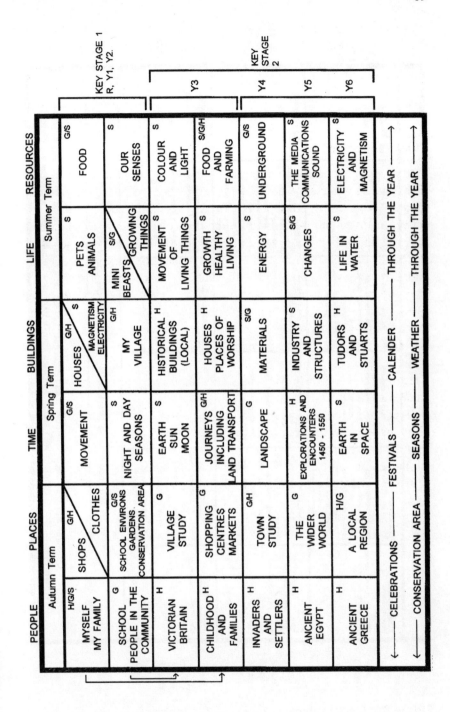

Figure 6.1: Key Stage Plan

	Autumn Term		Spring Term		Summer Term	
1st Year plan **Year A** Year 4 Year 5 Year 6	**Invaders and Settlers** Mapping places and invasions. The origin of settlements and reasons for location.	**Town Study** Living in an urban area. Why people move. Identify/investigate use of land and buildings, reasons for location. Links/relationships with other places. Land use activities. Sketches. Facilities available. Comparison with rural life	**Landscape** Identify/describe physical features and landforms. Contrasting landscapes. Earth movements. Natural Hazards. Climatic regions.	**Materials** Raw materials obtained from natural resources. How they are obtained from environment e.g. fishing, quarrying. Processing/transport. People's attitudes/effects on environment when extracting	**Energy** Conservation of fuel - pollution.	**Underground** Soils -different characteristics. Effect of relief
2nd Year plan **Year B** Year 4 Year 5 Year 6	**Ancient Egypt** Mapwork - location Agriculture of the Nile - irrigation. Farming compared with today.	**The Wider World** Case Study - Chembakolli (village). Comparison of food, culture, home work, transport, landscape, land use, leisure, natural vegetation. Case Study - Delhi (town)	**Explorations and Encounters** Trade routes. Navigation - points of compass. Continents, oceans, tropics, Equator. Different ways the globe can be represented.	**Industry and Structures** Industrial location.	**Changes** Pollution and how it effects us/what can be done? Conservation. Conflict over land use. How people have changed the environment. How damaged landscapes can be restored. Improving quality of own environment.	**The Media/Communication**
3rd Year plan **Year C** Year 4 Year 5 Year 6	**Ancient Greece** Mapwork - location Use of index/contents of atlas.	**Local Region** Maps, aerial photographs, location of activities/features in area. How jobs, land use, settlement pattern have been influenced by the area's environment/ location. Links with other places. Measuring straight line distances	**Earth in Space**	**Tudors and Stuarts** Mapwork - locating places	**Life in Water** Erosion/transportation/ deposition of materials by water. Features of a river system.	**Electricity/Magnetism**

Weather — Measure and record using direct observation and simple equipment.

Consider site conditions and how it can influence surface temperatures, wind speed and direction.
* Where ever possible, compare with another locality from Britain or a locality from a developing country.

Figure 6.2: Geographical components in topics
Key Stage Plan   Key Stage 2

Geography at Beaconside

LEA Report

High standards are being achieved in geography through well planned topic work. Though no teaching of the subject occurred during the inspection, outcomes of previous work provided ample evidence. The standard of work relating to geographical skills (AT1) and to physical and environmental geography (AT3, AT5) was particularly impressive. Evidence from pupils' work indicated a high quality of learning. Much is achieved through active involvement in tasks and activities which have clear learning objectives. The level of motivation achieved is high. Children show a real enthusiasm for their work and for the subject. They are encouraged to talk about and share their learning, bringing their own experiences of geography into the classroom. Equally a wide range of other adults visit classrooms to enrich the learning.

The assessment of children's progress is very thorough and has been carefully linked to National Curriculum requirements. Evidence of children's work is selected, dated, annotated and retained when it shows significant achievement. Attainment is recorded for each child against all five National Curriculum targets for geography. Staff are aware of the need to agree success criteria in order to standardise professional judgements of attainment. The school intends to use the non-statutory SATs for geography to assist this process.

Geography is planned as a component of cross curricular topic work. The degree of focus within each topic varies but balance is carefully monitored across the Key Stage. Staff are aware of the need to develop geographical skills sequentially wherever appropriate. Topics in all units provide practice in observation, recording and understanding of direction and plan view. Significant attention to environmental education is also evident, with a clear statement of aims for this aspect of learning alongside those for geography. Coverage of this and, less formally, of aspects of economic and industrial understanding, was seen in topics on pollution, in role play corners (shops) and in visits to places of work (local newspapers).

The development of a whole school policy statement is well advanced and includes the involvement of all colleagues. Careful monitoring for coverage will be required, particularly with aspects of the study of places and localities (AT2). The school is building upon valuable existing resources for the study of National Curriculum geography and is well placed to resource its intended active learning approach. An audit of current and future needs might usefully support the development of policy and practice and this could include the use made of environments beyond the classroom.

Figure 6.3

History (AT1, AT3)
Old photographs
Farming in the Lake
District

English (AT1, 2, 3, 4, 5)
Descriptive work
Tourism
Tourist Information Office
Acoustics

Geography (AT1, 2, 3)
Geology: looking at rocks and
glaciation
Looking at maps
Orienteering
Weather chart
Environmental issues – pollution, etc.

THE LAKE DISTRICT

RE
Feelings after a day out

Science (AT1, 2, 3, 2b)
Water, Ice
Penrith's water supply
Pumping station
Water wheels, water
power
Conservation

Music (AT1, AT2)
Water music
Handel's Water Music

Art (AT1, AT2)
Posters
Feltmaking

Maths (AT1, 2, 3, 4, 5)
LOGO
Timetables o'clock

Technology (AT1, AT4)
How can you get water
from A to B
Design and make a water wheel

PE
Climbing activities
Drama

Lakeland Artists,
e.g. Heaton Cooper,
John Campbell

Days of the week
Time sequence – re: journey
Number work

Figure 6.4: Year 1 Summer 1993

We started the topic by looking at the farming in the Lake District which is predominantly hill farming. We visited a hill farm in Mungrisdale where the children became very interested in the old farmhouse and the lambs and sheep. We looked at the different fleeces and skulls and the children learnt about all aspects of sheep farming, i.e. lambing, shearing, dipping, etc. We also looked at the cows and calves and how they were fed. We were able to see the various stages in the production of silage and slurry. After a visit the children produced observational drawings of skulls and stone walls and a 3D display of Ullswater and the Blencathra area showing a hill farm with clay models of sheep and lambs, farm buildings and models of the steamer, canoes, windsurfers and yachts on the lake. Visits from a local stonewaller and a wool spinner reinforced and further stimulated the children's enthusiasm.

A further visit included a ride on a steamer on Ullswater, a walk around Hallin Fell and a walk up to Aria Force. This outing produced various science activities such as the observation of a decaying tree with all its mini inhabitants, birdlife, and vegetation. At the foot of Aria Force one child was heard to remark, *'can it be turned off?'* *'Yes,'* said another, *'there's a tap at the top'.* *'No,'* said another, *'there's a drain where it all comes through'.* We climbed to the top to find out who was right.

We walked up the fellside and looked back at the glacial features of the area and had a display of local rocks in the classroom, sandstone, slate, limestone fossils, etc., which the children investigated independently first and then with a follow-up visit by a local geologist. We looked at local maps and the children drew their own maps of places we had visited. The children now have a much greater knowledge of the area in which they live.

'I learnt what the farm animals eat.'
'I learnt about being a farmer and how early they have to get up.'
'I learnt about sheep and farms and the Lake District fells.'
'I know we live near some lakes.'
'Water splashes all over and makes everything wet, it splashes on the rocks.'

Figure 6.5: Geography: Topic: The Lake District, Year 1.
(The class teacher's description)

Figure 6.6

TOWARDS A GEOGRAPHY POLICY
AIMS
1. To encourage children to become interested in and investigate their local environment.
2. To develop the skills and attitudes which enable children to conduct geographical investigations.
3. To increase knowledge and understanding about the local environment of Penrith and the surrounding area; about local economic and social activities, local physical features, and how people have affected the environment.
4. To give children a wider perspective and understanding of where they live, so that they begin to see their locality as a part of the UK and the rest of the world.
5. To develop understanding about physical processes, and how these affect landscape and human activities.

CURRICULUM ORGANIZATION
1. Geography will be introduced as part of the Unit Topics, integrated largely with other curriculum areas, and as an important part of the Environmental Education curriculum. Some Topics will be more appropriate than others for introducing geographical concepts and knowledge, and therefore the amount of geography in the curriculum will vary throughout the year.
2. Topic planning will take into account the Programmes of Study laid down in the NC document, and a balance of coverage will be aimed at over the three year period.
3. Some aspects of the knowledge requirements may be difficult to integrate into Topics, and may be taught separately, e.g. attention can be brought to the location of places in Britain and Europe during discussion of current news items, with appropriate maps used to draw children's attention to where places and physical features are situated.
4. Geography should be based on children's firsthand experience, and therefore will fit well with the school policy of using outside visits to introduce and reinforce learning experiences.

ASSESSMENT AND RECORDS
Geography will be continuously assessed from Reception onwards, and results of assessments recorded on the standard NC record sheets for individual pupils. Some Teacher Assessment Tasks should be incorporated into the Topic work when appropriate, to check particularly on the development of geographical skills and understanding.

The pupil profile report given to parents each Summer will contain reference to the child's progress in Geography, and at the end of Year 2 this will include the level of attainment.

Pupil records provide useful feedback to teachers about the effectiveness of teaching, and should be used to ensure that gaps in knowledge and understanding and geographical skills are filled before the end of the Key Stage.

Figure 6.6 *(continued)*

SUGGESTIONS FOR ACTIVITIES
1. Local visits to landmarks, shops, industries, etc.
2. Visits further afield, e.g. Bradford, Lake District, Carlisle, Northumberland, to provide comparisons and to extend experience.
3. Simple maps of coming to school, routes through town, farm maps, plans of buildings. Using keys.
4. Orienteering, following simple maps, e.g. Whinlatter.
5. Using photos of this and other localities, newspaper articles, TV news items, etc.
6. Talks from visitors, e.g. Antarctic explorers, National Park wardens, parents talking about their jobs, etc.
7. Using LOGO, PE, playground, compass, etc, to talk about directions.
8. Working in school grounds, improving habitats for wildlife and aesthetic appeal.
9. Using current news stories as a basis for discussion about pollution, etc.
10. Recycling activities in school, e.g. can bank. Energy saving measures.
11. Observations of weather.
12. Displays of rocks, etc.

RESOURCES
1. Information books on Geographical Topics – mainly available from school or County Library.
2. Maps – playmaps and jigsaws in Units 2 and 3, world, Europe, British Isles wall maps in Year 2 Unit.
3. Globes – inflatable large globes kept in PE store.
4. Photographs of physical features, weather phenomena, etc – kept in staffroom.
5. Guidelines for out-of-school visits – in Environmental Education support paper.
6. Background information – Curriculum support papers kept in staffroom.
7. Computer programmes – LOGO, Owl adventure, etc.
8. Playground markings.

Suggestions to take into account following the staff meeting to discuss Geography.

1. More use could be made of the school grounds, e.g.
   (i) following a map;
   (ii) making a map for others to follow;
   (iii) planning and creating improvements, e.g. the 'wild' area;
   (iv) adding to the playground, e.g. arrows to follow.
2. An adequate computer programme needs to be introduced in order that the children can create a database to record and review their findings.
3. AT2 Knowledge and understanding of places requires the children at Level 3 to compare our locality with another. It was felt that a comparison between the school locality and, for instance, the centre of the town would cover this statement adequately.
4. Opportunities should be taken to use events in the news, visitor's talks or children's own experiences in order to encourage them to find new places on a map.
5. Aerial photographs were felt to be a useful way to introduce the children to the idea of looking at an area from above.
6. The 1993 non-statutory SATs will be useful in defining the limits of Key Stage 1 and will help in interpreting the different levels.

Figure 6.7: Amendments following staff meeting – March 1993

CHAPTER 7

Beyond Locational Knowledge: Good Assessment Practice in Primary Geography

Bill Marsden

The Context: Returning to Meritocracy

Few, whether supporters or opponents of the National Curriculum, would dispute the fact that it is assessment-driven. Supporters would argue that this is a good thing, and opponents the reverse. The Thatcherite principles which underlie the National Curriculum are essentially nineteenth century meritocratic principles. Merit meant ability plus effort. At the time, advancement by merit was a socially progressive principle in that it replaced the previous system of family connection as the normal route to social and economic advance. It made it possible for capable and hard-working children from the respectable lower middle and upper working classes to become socially and economically upwardly mobile. It also involved competition with peers. The meritocratic ideology, however, had intrinsically an unacceptable face: it subscribed to an elitist survival of the fittest mentality, now undergoing a revival.

The implementation of the Education Reform Act (1988) is the culmination of a process going back to the confrontations between professional educators and the right-wing 'Black Paper' ideologues of the early 1970s. They campaigned against what they saw as a decline in educational standards, which they alleged had been implanted by the education industry during the permissive 1960s. This was the beginning of the shift from consensus to confrontational politics, in which the educational system has been embroiled ever since. This chapter is not about the broad political issues, nor about the associated social values, however, though these must form part of the context for any sensible discussion of assessment practice. Nor will it consider many of the aspects of bad practice that an assessment-led curriculum can encourage. It is rather about principles of *good practice in assessment* and how these can be applied to geography in the primary school, in the context of implementing the National Curriculum.

The Functions of Assessment

Assessment involves the gathering, recording, interpretation and use of information based on children's responses to educational tasks. At least four distinct functions of assessment can be identified (Harlen et al., 1992).

1 *Formative function:* usually through 'in-house' methods, providing vital feedback to teachers, pupils and parents on a continuing basis.

2 *Summative function:* usually through externally administered end of year or end of course tests or examinations, communicating publicly the results of pupils' achievements on the evidence of these tests.

3 *Certification function:* using the results of assessments, normally summative ones, for the purposes of selection and qualification.

4 *Quality Control function:* using aggregated information from assessments, again normally summative ones, as a means of judging the success of the teacher or department inside the school, or the school itself, or the local authority, to an external audience.

While it is important to take account of all these functions in the overall context, this chapter will concentrate on the first two.

Formative and Summative Assessment

At the heart of the conflicts of principle lie the distinctions between *formative* and *summative* assessment, and the purposes these are intended to serve.

Formative Assessment

Good formative assessment practice characteristically –

- is *continuing assessment* – an integral part of the learning process;
- measures children's performance against previously agreed criteria, and therefore is *criterion-referenced*;
- is the *responsibility of teachers*;

- is *shared with children,* building in negotiation and opportunity for self-assessment;
- is associated with carefully devised and regularly updated *records of achievement* offering a wide-ranging *profile* of progress made by the child to parents, other teachers, other schools and future employers;
- provides detailed and continuing *feedback on progress,* and thus is a basis for deciding what further learning is required;
- is *disaggregated,* that is it relates to one particular child and her or his progress, or lack of it;
- is related to *context,* such as the social and psychological factors affecting the individual child;
- makes possible a *value added* element, that is, appraises how much the individual child has progressed from her or his starting point.

Problems of Formative Assessment

It should not be assumed, however, that formative assessment by definition, or as of right, means good practice. There is good and bad formative assessment practice. There are some built-in problems.

- It is generally *subjective,* and can sometimes tell us more about teacher expectations than about pupil progress.
- Thus it can be *unreliable,* in that it will not give similar results if repeated in similar circumstances with a similar group of children at a later stage.
- It may also be *invalid,* that is, not assessing what it sets out to assess. For example, subjective assessments tend to give too much weight to *cosmetic* elements, such as neat presentation or good behaviour. Thus in progressive primary practice, what is regarded as good project display material may reflect presentational more than thinking skills, and be over-favourably assessed because it looks attractive. Work that is neatly copied out may falsely be offered as creative activity.
- Finally, formative assessment procedures have in some cases been held to be those most appropriate to less able children, with only the more able seen as fit to be entered for summative external assessments. This reflects a *deficit model* and low expectations.

Summative Assessment

Typically, summative assessment entails the *collection of new information.* It characteristically:

- is *'bolted-on'* at the end of an educational phase – usually the end of a year or the end of a course;

- is therefore *discontinuous* and detached from normal classroom activity;
- is often *externally administered,* and therefore detached from direct teacher influence; and,
- takes place on *special occasions* and in *abnormal settings* such as examination halls;
- is *not associated with detailed feedback*;
- is *norm-referenced,* that is, is related to a set of norms, or average performances, drawn from an appropriate population as a kind of benchmark against which children's responses can be measured.

Again, summative assessment is not bad *per se.* It is easier, for example, for summative assessment to meet some of the criteria of good assessment practice, such as *objectivity, reliability,* and *validity.* From the overall educational viewpoint, however, formative principles are those most conducive to promoting the natural, unforced development of the learning skills of the pupil. Clearly, current government thinking attaches less weight to these broader principles.

Principles of Good Practice in Assessment

1 Above all, good assessment must be associated with a set of agreed *educational aims and objectives.* These should be based on criteria of educational worth. Such criteria will relate both to worthwhile content and to worthwhile activities. Worthwhile assessment tasks will be based on children's normal work seen as an integral part of the process of improving learning. They should provide opportunities, at whatever level, for, for example:

    (a) *enquiry-based learning,* encouraging children to make informed choices on the basis of acquired skills and understandings, rather than merely to show the capacity to memorise and reproduce information;

    (b) *applying* these skills and understandings *in new situations*; and,

    (c) using these understandings and application skills in *problem-solving and creative activities.*

2 Good practice requires the use of a *range* of assessment instruments. Failure to observe this principle can lead to invalid judgements. Thus two children might have an equivalent grasp of a set of educational principles, but achieve differently because the limited and rigid assessment procedure adopted suited the learning style of one rather than the other. There is also evidence that some types of assessment suit boys rather than girls, and vice versa. The following assessment

procedures are available, and can be used appropriately for different purposes. They each have advantages and disadvantages.

- Extended writing, e.g. essays;
- Objective questions, e.g. multiple-choice items;
- Structured questions, as in many pencil and paper tests;
- Drawing (see Chapter 9);
- Extended projects, sometimes group-based;
- Oral assessment;
- Self-assessment.

3 Good practice in assessment should be related to relevant *theories of learning.* Two essential elements which need to be recognised and acted upon are:

- *differentiation*
- *progression.*

   (a) *Differentiation* can be promoted, for example, by using, as already suggested, a range of procedures which take account of different capacities. For example, in *structured questions,* there would be, in addition to a *core* element in the assessment for all children, further *reinforcement* activities for slower learners and *enrichment* activities to extend the work of the more able. Such procedures involve *differentiation by outcome* (the core task), followed by *differentiation by task* (the reinforcement and enrichment activities). Thus differentiated tasks will follow an initial task designed to diagnose ease or difficulty of understanding. Differentiation by task by itself, however, carries the danger of teachers being beguiled by preconceived notions of children's abilities and possible under- or over-expecting as to what they can achieve.

   (b) For *progression* to become part of the fabric, the assessment process needs to be integral to the total curriculum planning process, using a *spiral curriculum* model, the function of which is to enable children to return to concepts at progressively greater levels of refinement as they proceed through their schooling. An example of such a model is offered in Figure 7.1.

4 Good practice in assessment must promote *positive motivation.* One way of seeking this is to try to ensure that the *learning is successful,* which means *matching* the task effectively to the abilities and attitudes of the children. Relying on fear of failure is usually alienating, and as of principle is bad educational practice, whether formative or summative. Formative assessment, properly used, is more likely to be

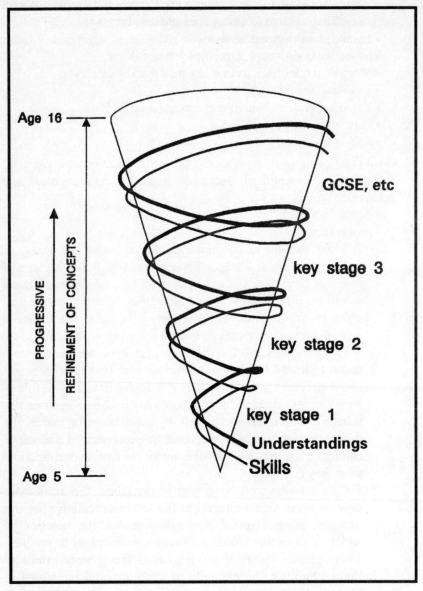

Figure 7.1: A spiral curriculum

a positive influence than summative, however, for by definition it keeps children regularly updated on their progress – vital in diagnosing and repairing the weaknesses and failures which lower motivation if left unchecked.

5 Good assessment practice involves regularly *reporting* a profile of achievement not only to the child but also the parent. The report needs to be meaningful to the parent as well as to the school. The parent as partner in the learning enterprise needs to be conversant with the frameworks and the language being used.

6 Good assessment practice, as already noted, is bound up with *context,* including social context. Almost by definition norm-referenced, summative assessment by external agencies aggregates and downplays context. Only by taking account of context can children – and for that matter, teachers and schools – be adequately and fairly appraised. Thus, knowledge of social and other contexts is vital in comparing one child with another. Competitive class lists giving tabulated rankings of children (and similarly league tables of schools) are context-free and are likely to do more harm than good, stimulating though they seem to be to those of the survival of the fittest mentality.

Does the National Curriculum Reflect Good Assessment Practice?

Here we must distinguish between the initial report of the Task Group of Assessment and Testing (TGAT) and the assessment procedures that emerged from the Education Reform Act of 1988. In general the TGAT team were experts on assessment procedures but were required to produce their report hastily. In the event the TGAT made recommendations later found too complex, time-consuming and expensive to implement. Following the anxieties expressed by SEAC on the one hand, and the panic responses of right-wing pressure groups on the other, the government backtracked. A more limited and reactionary assessment policy was promoted, giving primacy to externally produced Standard Assessment Tasks (SATS). It remained cautious and sceptical about teacher assessments (TAS). While this is still the basic position, pragmatic considerations have moved the government in the direction of restricting the full rigour of SATS to the core subjects.

In general, current government thinking about assessment reflects bad educational practice on a whole series of grounds.

1 It is based on a meritocratic, competitive, even combative view of the world, setting one school against another in the interests of supposed

quality control, demanding that schools play the examinations game. The backwash effect of this 'high stakes' element on teaching and learning is likely to be reactionary – the assessment tail wagging the curriculum dog.

2 The back to basics thinking extolled by government, at worst fosters a 'trivial pursuits' approach to knowledge. While to most people in education, knowledge and understanding represent high level educational objectives, in official circles they seem to mean, for history and geography, acquiring and recalling basic facts such as dates of battles and the reigns of monarchs, and the names of capital cities.

3 The official recommendations relate to no accepted *theory of learning*. Therefore the crucial 'levels' of the National Curriculum – supposed to promote progression – are, in subjects such as geography and science, couched in content terms rather than being tied to levels of understanding. They do not reflect the vital point that knowledge and understanding are keys to fostering higher level intellectual skills, and that the levels should essentially be related to the development of these skills. The essence of progression in learning is to revisit the same concepts and key ideas in different situations and at more complex and refined levels of understanding. This cannot be done where one set of concepts is deemed suitable for one National Curriculum level, and another for a later one.

4 Additionally, the statements of attainment in subjects like science and geography are too numerous and too specific. It is potentially valuable that the post-Dearing statements are broader. It is hoped they can be built into a framework of progression. This would involve a return to the ideas of a *spiral curriculum,* in which the basic principles and concepts of geography are revisited at different stages, matched as appropriate to pupils' levels of understanding (Figure 7.1).

Good Assessment Practice in Primary Geography

Good assessment practice in primary geography, it follows, will reflect the specific application of the above principles of good assessment practice in general. There are of course a number of additional subject-specific principles. The overriding one is that good assessment in geography will be *distinctively geographical,* reflecting:

(a) its distinctive *skills,* particularly related to map interpretation; and
(b) its key educational function as a *visual subject*;
and, in respect of *content,*
(c) its focus on *place*;

(d) its responsibility as the main National Curriculum subject contributing to *global study.*

A Case Study of a Curriculum Plan in Primary Geography and its Assessment

Assessing Mountains

This plan reflects a compromise between three basic needs:

(i) to meet the requirements of the National Curriculum;
(ii) to promote and follow good assessment practice;
(iii) to promote and follow good geographical practice.

Before you think about assessment, a curriculum plan relating to your chosen topic is needed. In this case we will be following the principles of a spiral curriculum. Imagine that as a primary geography co-ordinator, you work in a school in an upland region and, having visited and become interested in mountain regions in other areas, and with many resources as well as the experience at your disposal, you decide that the *Geography of Mountain Areas* is to be a major theme in your curriculum plan.

(i) Consulting the geography programmes of study, you will find that there are many opportunities for linking such a theme with the different strands of the National Curriculum, not only in physical geography, but also between this and human geography and environmental geography. By definition, in a distinctively geographical scheme, the thematic material will be linked also with skills and studies of places.
(ii) In terms of *progression,* the idea will be to revisit the theme of mountains, say at three stages:
   Infant (Key Stage 1, Levels 2/3)
   Lower Junior (Key Stage 2, Levels 3/4)
   Upper Junior (Key Stage 2, Levels 4/5).

Remember that *revisiting means reinforcement and not repetition.* It is important that children do not feel they are doing the same thing over and over again.

The plan of campaign is illustrated on the spiral curriculum diagram (Figure 7.1). This is based on the following fundamental geographical and educational principles:

(a) a case study, place-based approach;
(b) a concentric approach, moving out from the local mountain area, say the Cairngorms, to the European then the global setting, using the Alps and Himalayas respectively from which to select localities for study;
(c) linkage of geographical skills, areas and themes, thus not treating physical geography in isolation, but showing its interdependence with places

and human and environmental themes;

(d) the building in of progression, beginning with initial awareness of concepts, then extending and enriching them in order to move on to more complex and refined understandings.

Methods of Assessing the Mountains Unit

It is clearly beyond the scope of this chapter to cover the forms of assessment appropriate to all the elements of the above scheme. Here, a sample of representative issues of assessment will be addressed, as appropriate to different levels of the spiral curriculum.

(a) Basic Understanding: Exploring Geographical Vocabulary

The old-fashioned way of dealing with geographical vocabulary was to learn definitions off by heart. This is poor educational practice because it generates little more than 'trivial pursuits' knowledge – factual information without meaning. It is important to accept that a definition of knowledge confined to the ability to recall basic facts is an extremely confining one. It is crucial to link knowledge with understanding, as a means of access to the staircase of ever deepening intellectual abilities. The first steps on the staircase are to do with basic awareness. How do we establish whether a child can understand something *at the level of initial awareness?* One method is to see whether she or he can *distinguish exemplars from non-exemplars* of a particular concept.

Thus a *mountain,* being a general term, is also a *concept.* The preliminary awareness of children about what mountains are may come through direct personal observation if living in a mountainous area, or through indirect experience from observation of photographs, picture maps and drawings.

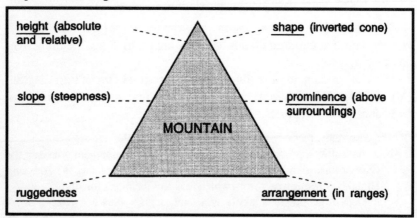

Figure 7.2: Mountains: Basic attributes (concepts)

Mountains are distinguished, in dictionary definitions, by such attributes as:

— height
— steepness of slopes
— sharp cone-shape.

It would be a sign of *progression* if the child could then verbally or in

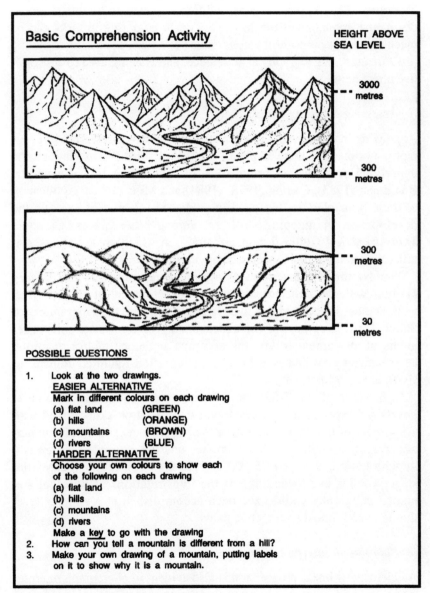

Figure 7.3: Assessing mountains

writing give reasons or the criteria by which he or she identified the feature as a mountain – for example, by labelling the drawing appropriately.

Such basic understanding can conveniently be assessed through different types of pencil and paper test. Such tests should not be dismissed as intrinsically limiting. They can be judged good or bad according to whether they promote particular worthwhile educational objectives. Thus Figure 7.3 asks children to colour in two diagrams to distinguish mountains from hills. Obviously colouring in tasks can be mechanical, but purposeful colour coding is a form of classification and identification, in geography as in science, and is being used to constructive effect here.

(b) Assessing Mapping Skills

Appraising mapping skills is a fundamental task of assessment in geography. Fortunately, there is plenty of well-established case-law on the underlying principles of progression in mapping as in, for example, Boardman (1983), Catling (1978) (1984) and Mills (1988). Application of these principles can be found in published schemes of work on the development of mapping skills in, among other places, Catling's *Mapstart* series (Collins/Longman, 1992), in which graded assessment tasks are offered in the associated copymasters.

The National Curriculum Working Group was obviously very familiar with the basic research on the development of skills in map work and has introduced this in a reputable way into the Programmes of Study. Thus, in respect of the understanding of coordinates, the statements of attainment follow the accepted sequence of, for example, letter/number coordinates at Level 3 through four-figure coordinates to six-figure coordinates at Level 5.

In the case of the 'Mountains' theme, there could therefore be at Levels 4/5 assessment of formal map interpretation skills linked with assessment of the understanding of the physical geography of a mountain region, together with its impact on, for example, routeways, through questions on a 1:25 000 or 1:50 000 O.S. map. At an earlier stage, similar understandings of the inter-relations of physical and human geography could have been accomplished at a simpler level through tasks linked with picture maps.

(c) Photograph Interpretation

An element of linear progression is also evident in photograph interpretation, with different stages relatively easy to recognise, as is evident in the Statutory Orders.

- Simple pictures of familiar places taken from ground level, as on family or teacher photographs or postcards (Level 1).
- Simple then more complex pictures of unfamiliar settings which can be used for comparison with familiar places (Level 2/3).
- Oblique aerial photographs (Level 3).
- Vertical aerial photographs (Level 4).

A useful way of helping children to interpret photographs is to ask them to label features on them. Diagnosis of levels of recognition and understanding can also be achieved by grids of questions attached to the photograph, with arrows from the relevant points on the photograph leading to the questions round the edge. Photograph interpretation forms a very good basis for structured questions as well.

(d) Structured questions

Structured questions are a transition form between objective items such as multiple-choice tests, and extended writing. They are widely used at all stages of schooling and in most if not all subjects. They are often in the form of pencil and paper tests which, as already indicated, can represent good or bad assessment practice. One advantage of structured questions is their flexibility. As discussed earlier, it offers a core activity, which enables diagnosis of whether children have achieved a basic awareness of simple concepts associated with the physical and human geography of a mountain region. Children not yet able to work at this level need to be referred to a simpler task, perhaps another picture with less complex landscape information included.

(e) Creative Work and its Assessment

The educational need to place the emphasis on developing the skills of understanding should not divert us from the complementary requirement to use the world's environments to foster creative activity – whether writing, drawing, or more ambitious media work, such as the presentation of annotated photomontages, or poetry, simulations, or stories. Let us take one example of a geographically oriented story about a mountain region. It was in the form of a project in creative writing and drawing. The children were divided into groups and each group had to produce one part of an *illustrated and sequenced story* about a skiing accident in the mountains. The work the children produced was diagnostic not only of creative abilities, but also of geographical levels of understanding, which could complement more strictly geographical approaches to the theme. So far as the permeation of geographical material was concerned, the following evidence of knowledge and understanding was apparent:

- basic concepts about the shape of mountains;
- association of mountains with a particular area (in this case the Austrian Alps);
- association of mountains with particular shapes and styles of houses (steeply pitched wooden chalet type);
- association of mountains with wooded slopes;
- association of mountains with snow and hazards such as avalanches and icy roads;
- association of mountains with human activities such as tourism and, in this case, skiing;
- link with rescue services.

Such work also introduces an important *attitudinal dimension,* central to successful work in issues-based geography. It could additionally have been linked with environmental problems.

Non-Statutory SATS in Geography

As Blyth (1990, p.83) has illustrated, meeting the needs of National Curriculum assessment can be addressed at different levels, each more rigorous (or pseudo-rigorous) than the next.

1 In the first place there is the everyday informal appraisal of the children by the classroom teacher on the basis of systematic observation and recording.

2 This may be associated with concurrent assessment of the products of the child's work through answers to different types of questions on worksheets, or in exercise books.

3 Then there are the more formal teacher assessments demanded by the National Curriculum which in future will presumably require external moderation. These may be based on non-statutory SATs.

4 Finally there are the formal SATS now to be restricted to the core subjects.

Thus the most 'rigorous' form of National Assessment for geography will presumably be staged teacher assessment, building on the principles contained in non-statutory SATS. These have now appeared for Key Stage 1 (SEAC, 1993). We have had for some time clues about their nature, for earlier statutory SATS in science were associated with topics overlapping with geography, in particular with weather. The non-statutory SATS in geography do not differ greatly from this model. An example is given in Chapter 9 (Figure 9.2) of the use in SATS of children's drawings as diagnostic of their understanding of an aspect of weather study in science.

One advantage claimed for the non-statutory SATS is that they have been tested out in schools. One disadvantage is that pencil and paper tests in themselves are often generalised and fail to create the sense of a place element that is at the heart of authentic geographical study. It is important to avoid mere comprehension exercises offered in the guise of geography. It is therefore encouraging that at least some real photographs of respectable quality have been included in the non-statutory SATS for geography at Key Stage 1.

It is also surely a boon that SATS for geography will not be statutory. This gives teachers more flexibility in devising their own appraisals, and the opportunity to harness a wide range of assessment instruments in probing children's geographical understandings, which means in turn developing skills of assessment, not least in making it varied and an integral part of the process of curriculum planning. As we have seen, some aspects of the National Curriculum Statements of Attainment reflect bad assessment practice. But while they may inhibit good practice they do not prevent it taking place. Indeed the National Curriculum in geography has left many gaping holes and grey areas which can be exploited by resourceful teachers anxious to continue to promote good geographical and progressive assessment practice, while not neglecting the demands of Statutory Orders.

PART C

Links

CHAPTER 8

Geography through Information Technology: Supporting Geographical Enquiry

Ashley Kent and Andy Philips

The Opportunity

The incorporation of information technology (any system which enhances the ability of individuals to obtain, handle and communicate information in the areas of computing, broadcasting, telecommunications and printing) in the National Curriculum is for England and Wales a unique recognition of its educational importance. Information Technology is specified in both the geography National Curriculum Order and the Technology Order. In the geography Programmes of Study for Key Stages 1 and 2, pupils 'should be given opportunities to use IT'.

As the non-statutory guidance for geography (NCC, 1991) puts it, 'strong links exist between geography and IT. IT encourages pupils to handle information more effectively, to pose and test hypotheses, to communicate and present the results of geographical enquiries and to measure and collect data about the environment'. The non-statutory guidance goes on to ask teachers of geography to consider the following:

Current provision – what IT experiences do pupils have at present in geography?

IT planning – what further opportunities are there for using IT?

Continuity and progression – how does the use of IT in geography, build on and support the use of IT in other subjects and Key Stages?

Resources – how can resources – hardware, software and staff expertise – be best allocated to provide IT for pupils? Classroom management and group work can overcome many problems associated with limited access to hardware.

Review – what are the procedures to record, monitor and assess and evaluate the pupils' IT capability?

As the non-statutory guidance for Wales puts it, there are a number of ways in which IT can enhance learning in geography. It can for example:

— improve the quality of pupils' geographical experiences;
— enable pupils, including those with learning difficulties, to work at their own pace while also providing stimulating extension exercises for the most able;
— enable pupils to process data easily, thus allowing the opportunity to concentrate on understanding and awareness. (CCW, 1991)

Official approval for the incorporation of IT within geography lessons seems to have been given as the above suggests, but it has been argued that both the final geography Order and Programmes of Study gave little specific and statutory encouragement (Kent, 1992) for this. The fear is that IT within geography may therefore be seen as low priority (and indeed optional) given a geography Order considered by some to be overloaded in content.

The technology Order gives no such option for teachers. Information Technology Capability, according to its non-statutory guidance (NCC, 1990) concerns:

• knowledge about applications of IT and about IT tools such as word processors, databases, spreadsheets, and software for processing sound and images;
• the skill to use appropriate IT tools effectively;
• an understanding of the new opportunities IT provides;
• knowledge of the effects and limitations of IT.

Figure 8.1 lists the five strands of IT capability and gives examples for each of them.

Figure 8.1

What is IT Capability in Geography?

This is a pupil's ability to operate effectively and creatively with IT. It is the building of confidence and competence through the strands of IT capability across the whole range of National Curriculum subjects and cross-curricular themes. The strands of IT capability are:

(1) Communicating information
(2) Handling information
(3) Modelling
(4) Measurement and control
(5) Evaluating applications and effects.

Communicating geographical ideas and information involves:	word processing desk-top publishing graphing concept keyboard packages multi-media presentation electronic mail
Handling geographical information involves:	databases spreadsheets on-line and viewdata concept keyboard packages CD–ROM and AIV
Modelling geographical situations involves:	adventures simulations spreadsheets
Controlling, measuring and collecting geographical data involves:	programmable devices automatic weather stations data loggers satellite images
Evaluating geographical effects involves:	IT at home IT at work IT in economically developing countries IT in weather prediction

---

The non-statutory guidance for IT Capability (NCC, 1990) states that the primary school teacher is responsible for the individual child's IT experiences:

• using IT to enhance learning;
• developing each pupil's IT capability in accordance with school policy;
• ensuring that each pupil has access to IT resources;

• monitoring and evaluating pupils' experiences;
• determining the next stage in each pupil's use of IT, and ensuring continuity and rigour;
• contributing to each pupil's record of development.

Case Studies

Each of the case studies included in this section has been chosen for the way it can be used with children of differing ages and abilities. It is not always necessary for sophisticated geography work to be accompanied by high level use of technology. In the examples used here, the technology is specifically to support and enhance the geographical work undertaken by the pupils.

Case Study 1

'Weather Watch'

Two schools, one in eastern England and the other on the west coast decided to form links in order that both teachers and pupils could exchange information on life in both localities. Classes were twinned and a consensus was reached over which topics and themes the two schools would collaborate.

One such topic was 'Weather and its effect on our daily lives'. Both schools had access to standard weather equipment (rain gauge, maximum and minimum thermometers and a wind vane/anemometer) which enabled them to record simultaneously the weather on a daily basis, including: maximum temperature, minimum temperature, precipitation, wind direction and speed.

After faxing a copy of the completed recording sheet to their twin school, each school entered both sets of records into a database for analysis. They interrogated this data to compare and contrast the weather between the two localities; on what days did most rain fall and was it the same day for each school; were the highest temperatures recorded at the same time; and were temperatures significantly different between the two localities?

What particularly interested the pupils was that the weather in the two localities was often the same except that it occurred at either different times of the same day, or there was an even longer delay between the school on the east coast experiencing the rain that the west coast school had already measured and recorded. From this exercise the pupils were beginning the first stages of being able to follow weather charts and to understand that weather systems move in different directions across the country. They were also able to see the value of using technologies to transmit this information and so develop an understanding of how weather forecasts are aided by such information.

IT Strand: Handling Information.
Software/Hardware needed: Fax machine.

Case Study 2

'One World Week'

As part of a whole school topic on 'Our World', each class studied a different country, with the whole school covering a range of Economically Developing Countries. Each morning they undertook work related to their chosen country and in the afternoon the children took it in turns to 'visit' one of the other countries being studied by the other classes. In preparation for their visitors, each class was encouraged to prepare a travel brochure advertising some of the distinctive features of their country. The pupils used desk-top publishing software to prepare their brochures. Some of the classes printed out their copy from FRONT PAGE EXTRA and glued on colour pictures whilst some pupils used NEWSPA which allowed them to scan in colour photographs taken by one of the teachers on a recent holiday.

IT Strand: Communicating Information.
Software/Hardware needed: any Desk-Top Publishing package.

Case Study 3

'Changing our Town Centre'

As part of an investigation into the proposed development of a pedestrian precinct in their local town centre, one class of pupils decided to ask local residents and shopkeepers their views on this issue. They began by asking other pupils and teachers in the school their opinions on this matter. Armed with clipboards and questionnaires the pupils went out into the town centre (with their teacher and accompanying adults) to gauge local opinion. So diverse were the views of different groups within the community that the class teacher thought that this issue would make for an ideal planning enquiry. The class were divided into groups with each one being given a different interest group to represent: old age residents; families with young children; shopkeepers; teenagers; and the Save the Town Centre Association. To prepare for the enquiry, each group was asked to produce a publicity sheet outlining the main arguments that they wanted to present.

Much thought and attention was paid to both the content and layout of their sheet as each group was most concerned that it presented its points of view very concisely and clearly. They learnt a lot about how newspapers and publishers work in terms of ensuring that the layout and style as well as the message are very important in influencing and attracting the readers.

IT Strand: Communicating Information.
Software/Hardware needed: Word Processing or Desk-Top Publishing package.

Case Study 4

'Planning a Housing Estate'

A class of pupils in Sheffield was interested to discover that a local property developer was keen to build a housing estate on a field adjacent to their school. On obtaining a proposed plan of the site, they visited the field to gain some understanding of the effect that this development would have on both the existing traffic networks and local residents. They were also very interested in both the number and style of buildings being proposed as well as leisure facilities. Back at school they cut out a plan of the site on graph paper and using 'Monopoly' pieces as an indicator of different housing types (detached, semi-detached, maisonette) they set about developing their own plans.

The developer had given them the estimated prices for both building and selling the various types of houses, as well as an indication as to what roads, pavements, gas, electricity and water supplies would cost. Using this information the teacher was able to create a spreadsheet into which the pupils entered the number of each house type they wanted to build. On entering all relevant information the spreadsheet calculated whether they would make a profit or loss. They realised that whilst BMX tracks and adventure playgrounds would make the site very popular with young children it was not going to be in the best interests of, for instance, the developer, who could make more money by building houses instead.

IT Strand: Modelling.
Publisher: Home Sweet Home, Northern Micro-Media.
Software/Hardware needed: Spreadsheet package.

Case Study 5

'The Jolly Postman'

The children in one school had been reading the story of *The Jolly Postman* by A. and J. Allberg, as a way of understanding directional language. With the teacher's help the children had made a model of the village showing the various houses in which the characters lived. These were laid out on the floor of the classroom and the pupils had to direct a ROAMER (the postman) to each one of the houses in order to deliver the letters. Working in groups the pupils drew a map that the ROAMER had to use to get from the post office to their character's house which they annotated with distances and direction. Very soon they were able to programme the ROAMER so that it was able to get from the post office to the appropriate house by the shortest route. All the while the children were developing confidence in using geographical vocabulary to direct the device.

IT Strand: Measurement and Control.
Software/Hardware needed: ROAMER or other programmable device.

Case Study 6

'Setting up in Business'

As part of an investigation into the uses of IT in the high street, pupils visited an estate agency to ask the manager how IT helps her to run her business. The manager explained that the details of each house are entered into a database using a range of fields including: age, style, bedrooms, garage, bathrooms, garden and price. Each new client visits the office and then types in his or her requirements; the software calls up all those properties which match the needs of the client.

IT Strand: Applications and Effect.
Publisher: Home Sweet Home, Northern Micro-Media.
Software/Hardware needed: Data-handling package.

The Challenge

For the DfE, SCAA and CCW to make such statements in Orders and non-statutory guidance is one thing, but for all this to happen is another! A certain amount of research has been undertaken to determine the present level of IT across the curriculum. It will come as no surprise to educators that there is a gap between the expectations of the National Curriculum and present reality in schools.

A DfE conference on Primary IT, held in October 1992, drew attention to the 'spectacular progress in the use of IT in primary schools in the past ten years' and referred to HMIs comment that there were 'grounds for considerable satisfaction with the progress of IT in primary schools'. However, HMI also observed that 'teachers remained tentative, did not always intervene appropriately and were insecure in making judgements about pupils' attainment'. While more schools had IT policies, many (70%) were ineffective. IT featured in the curriculum planning of most teachers but usually only in terms of the activity to be undertaken. Reported at the same conference was that 'many teachers had real difficulty with other strands of IT – notably modelling, control, and applications and effects'.

Clearly the hardware and software situation has improved for primary schools but they are still a good way behind the resourcing of secondary schools, though the resource gap is narrowing. In 1990 for instance there were 4.3 micros per primary school with £1,000 spent on IT whereas in 1992 the respective figures were 7 and £2,300. These average figures, however, clearly hide a very uneven distribution of resources across the country. Most lessons observed by HMI with any IT content were using word processing, but the other IT strands were rarely incorporated.

Other research has pointed to the relatively low levels of IT skills, experience and confidence in those embarking on Primary PGCE courses (Mellar and Jackson, 1992; Wild and Hodgkinson, 1992) as well as for experienced teachers. Murray (1992) states that 'results of a survey indicate that primary school teachers lack sufficient understanding, of the concepts involved, (i.e. re: IT capability) to translate guidelines into practice!'

Certainly the largest and most comprehensive research into the state of IT was undertaken by the ImpacT Project (1993). This evaluated the impact of IT on children's achievements in primary and secondary schools, 'thereby assessing the extent to which the investment had delivered widely the 'educational value' which had been shown in schools committed to IT.' 'The research findings pointed to great inconsistencies in IT's contribution to learning across subjects and age groups.' Case studies of 14–16 year olds in geography classrooms were undertaken but, 'the project was unable to identify a satisfactory sample for geography in the primary cohort!' (ImpacT, 1993). 'Many teachers and LEAs may espouse the regular use of IT but it is rarely actually happening in classrooms' (Watson, 1993). The broad findings of ImpacT have substantial policy implications and this may well explain recent DfE initiatives taken in 1993. 'Most schools still do not provide enough access to computers for pupils; pupils need explicit opportunities to learn to work effectively in a collaborative environment; the implementation of IT activities is primarily dependent on individual teacher's initiatives; teachers' particular pedagogic skills and understandings of geography appeared to influence their use of IT; these teachers do not have enough time or planned opportunities in which to share their experiences with their colleagues; there are real problems rationalising the content requirements of the NC with the process and more open-ended aspects of certain highly valued, activities using IT!'

As to the teaching of geography at primary level, it is probably significant that the HMI report (1989) which declared that 'overall standards of work in geography were very disappointing' made no mention of the use of IT in its general description of geography though some mention of good practice observed was made in the section on 'teaching and learning'. The section on 'modern technology' uses exhortation rather than praise as a tactic. OFSTED (1993) in their review of the first year of National Curriculum Geography in Key Stages 1 and 2 note that 'little use was made of information technology (IT)...in geography teaching'.

Emerging Technologies

A good deal of futurology (and a good deal of it rhetoric) is enjoyed in the IT field. It started with Papert as early as 1980 and has continued ever since. Allen, quoted in Kent (1992), employed a panel of 24 'experts' to look at 2000AD through their crystal balls. They envisaged a future where IT would play an emancipatory role for pupils and 'the most significant change predicted by the experts is the greatly increased use of word processors by pupils'. Riley (1992) suggested that 'notebook computers may become as commonplace as calculators in schools'. Our experience with portable computers is certainly increasing and an important DfE funded project on portable computers for schools and teacher training announced in January 1993 and reporting in 1994 published an interim report recently (NCET, 1993).

The National Council for Educational Technology (NCET) held a series of seminars in December 1992 addressing the future with IT. A discussion report was published in August 1993 (NCET, 1993). In particular, Peter Seaborne, under the heading 'The picture of IT use in schools', considered there was now a need to:

- identify what progression in IT competence is about – in relation to pupils who have grown up with IT;
- consider the consequences of increasing hardware in classrooms – for teachers, the teaching environment and the way it is organised;
- enable all teachers to pass through the 'pain' threshold to confidence with IT;
- address the question of what is the best use of teachers' expertise – what teachers should be doing in the educative process and what can be done in other kinds of ways.

Three specific and relatively recent emerging technologies are beginning to impact on geography teaching at all levels. These are CD–ROM, multi-media and remote sensing. The impact of read only compact discs (CD–ROM) in the geography curriculum is increasing as discs containing climatic data, atlas information and country profiles are being produced. More discs are becoming available at the same time as the price of the technology is falling. Multi-media allows the user to collate and present information in a way undreamt of ten years ago. An early example of the opportunities this application offers the geography teacher can be found in the Project HIT publication *Multi-Media in History and Geography.* The geography National Curriculum offers opportunities where considerable benefit can be gained from the use of remotely sensed images. Key Stage 2 Programmes of Study requires pupils to use aerial photography for instance. Happily for teachers of geography, various resources are now available. In particular the Remote Sensing in the Geography National Curriculum Project (RSGP) has been at work since 1992 producing two packs, one for primary teachers (KS2), the other for secondary teachers (KS3 and 4). The Geographical Association is to publish these packs in the Autumn 1994. The primary pack consists of the following:

Four booklets –

— introduction to aerial photographs and satellite images
— using aerial photographs and satellite images in primary classrooms
— St Lucia (linking to Geographical Association/Worldaware pack)

— comprehensive resource section on availability of aerial photographs and satellite images, and supporting materials and agencies.

Twelve colour images – including Loch Torridon, Brazilian rain-forest and Kano.

Eight black and white images – including large aerial photographs of Castries, in St Lucia.

Three posters – including London Docklands and Cambridge-shire.

The purpose of the pack is to:

- explain remote sensing and image analysis in suitable terms;
- provide activities for teachers to help them gain confidence with imagery;
- provide images with materials and examples of classroom activities;
- suggest ideas and activities for INSET sessions;
- report on examples of good practice;
- inform teachers of the availability of images, resources and IT.

Resources to support the teacher

A good deal of help is now available for the teacher. Early practical support was the Learning Geography with Computers INSET Pack (NCET, 1989).

Although it is focused on Key Stages 3 and 4 geography it offers considerable possibilities for those teaching KS2. For instance, two of the case studies on data handling using GRASS (a data handling package) are for top juniors. Similarly the two booklets from the Geographical Association/NCET(1992) entitled *Geography, IT and the National Curriculum* have several KS3 and 4 examples adaptable to KS2. *Using Computers in Fieldwork* (1988) is similar but *Geography Through Topics in Primary and Middle Schools* (Mills, 1989) is full of IT applications.

The Geographical Association's continuing involvement at the Association's annual conferences and BETT (the major IT in education annual conference) conferences, through workshops for primary teachers, has been a considerable support. Its publication, *Primary Geographer,* has had an IT section since its first issue in Spring, 1989. Figure 8.2 shows the focus of some of the IT sections of *Primary Geographer,* edited by Des Bowden. In addition it incorporates regular software reviews.

Several individuals on the Geographical Association's information technology working group such as Helen Warner *(Journal of Computer*

Figure 8.2

A Selection from *Primary Geographer's* IT Section

Spring, 1989	Satellites and the primary school
	'Enjoying your computer'
Spring, 1990	Concept Keyboard
Spring, 1991	Data Handling
Autumn, 1991	Geography and IT in a reception class
Summer, 1992	Spreadsheets
October, 1993	Geography Software (general piece)
January, 1993	Datalogging

Assisted Learning, 1990 – a piece on LOGO and geography), and Keith Paterson (developed with colleagues a Ladakh Pack including a useful database) have supported the cause of primary geography and IT. The NCET produces an annual resources catalogue (1993) and has a helpful information room which fields enquiries about software and other resources for primary geography and IT. In particular, *Making Links* (1992) is a pack available from NCET helping teachers integrate IT with history and geography at Key Stage 2. Another NCET Project is HIT (Humanities and Information Technology Project) which since 1988 has helped develop the use of IT in history, geography and some of the cross-curricular themes.

Ways Forward

Overall, as implied by some of the ImpacT Project's findings, in spite of some progress over the last ten years or so in bringing IT across the curriculum, classroom activity has been disappointing. The National Curriculum has given a boost to geography taught through IT and also there have been various publications and initiatives to reinforce that impetus. For instance, Project INTENT (NCET, 1993) the Initial Teacher Education and New Technology Project 1990–2 had a focus on staff development for tutors in order to integrate the use of IT across courses and prepare all students to use IT effectively in their teaching of pupils. Similarly, again funded by NCET was the publication, *Making IT Happen* (NCET, 1991) which reviewed some of the issues which need to be addressed by policy makers in institutes of higher education. Similarly, *Focus on IT* (NCET, 1991) for Key Stages 1, 2 and 3 is a pack of materials aimed to help schools develop some of the knowledge, skills and techniques necessary to plan the effective development of IT capability for their pupils.

However, amidst this general 'boosterism' there is a need to retain a critical eye on all these developments. These include:

• a concern that children will interact more with machines than with people;
• a concern that IT (the tail) may too readily wag the geography curriculum 'dog';
• a concern for the opportunity costs of these IT developments;
• a concern that the vocational relevance of IT programmes below graduate level is often overplayed;
• a concern that educators and their educational objectives are powerless in the face of a powerful computer/industrial lobby;
• a concern that an extension of IT can reinforce power, extending exploitation and control;
• a concern that there seems to be increasing polarization between children in certain schools with a richness of IT experience (e.g. City Technology Colleges or TVEI schools) and those in less favourable circumstances. Is the logical extension of this a majority of IT illiterate and deskilled pupils and a minority of powerful IT literate?
• a concern for gender imbalance in the ways IT across the curriculum is delivered in schools.

Notwithstanding such cautions the impetus is certainly for further encouragement of IT in all geography classrooms. Recent GEST funding arrangements for 1994/5 allow the possibility of advisory support and in-service training and equipment, software and materials to encourage IT in certain subject areas including geography. Furthermore, over £100,000 of DfE funding is to be spent on a Project Officer and regional initiatives steered by the Geographical Association to encourage further integration of IT in geography courses. In addition to this the DfE announced in February 1994 the CD–ROM in Primary Schools initiative. Many of the 22 titles supported by this scheme will enhance pupils' experience of geography in the primary school. This momentum is still far from being spent.

Useful addresses

National Council for Educational Technology (NCET), Science Park, University of Warwick, Coventry CV4 7EZ.
(NCET has produced a comprehensive directory of software for schools, EDUCATIONAL SOFTWARE.)

GA ITWG (IT Working Group), The Geographical Association, 343 Fulwood Road, Sheffield S10 3BP.

The Advisory Unit, Computers in Education, 126 Great North Road, Hatfield AL9 5J2.

Project HIT (Humanities and Information Technology), University of London, Institute of Education, 20 Bedford Way, London WC1H 0AL.

MAPE (Micros and Primary Education), Newman College, Bartley Green, Birmingham B32 3NT.

The Remote Sensing in the Geography National Curriculum Project (RSGP), Institute of Education, University of London, 20 Bedford Way, London WC1H 0AL.

The following are also of use

LIST EXPLORER is available from NCET (address above).

Concept Keyboards. *For further information on their use contact:* The Concept Keyboard Company Ltd, Moorside Road, Winnall Industrial Estate, Winchester, Hants SO23 7RX.

CHAPTER 9

Linking Geography with History and Art: a Focused Topic Work Approach

Bill Marsden

Background

A source of concern to HMI (DES, 1978, 1989) and to educational writers such as Alexander (1984), was the ill-focused topic work frequently found in primary schools. While HMI noted satisfactory or better topic work in many schools, it was pointed out that the subjects most usually associated with this approach, such as geography and history, were those least well served by it. In most schools geography, even where it was present, lost its distinctiveness. At worst, the geography and history element consisted largely of copying notes and illustrations related to the topics under consideration. The gains made from the approach were rather in the opportunities it offered for practising skills in language and art.

One of the main reasons for the ill-focused quality of much integrated work has been the widely used brainstorming approaching, with its characteristically promiscuous end-product of a topic-web. If brainstorming is merely the preliminary stage of a planning process, later to be refined by careful weeding and the seeking out of connections, then no harm is done. The potential problems, however, were not just in the minds of HMI. For example:

(a) Where does the topic-web stop? This is less of a problem in a restricted local study. But where the intention is, for example, to build the study up to a global scale, or where a broad cross-disciplinary theme such as transport is covered, then brainstorming is prone to offer a confusing tangle of ideas, as overloaded with content as any Statements of Attainment in the National Curriculum.

(b) From this it follows that the 'web' is endemically a *collection* of ideas, rather than a carefully planned structure which supplies the coherent conceptual *connections* necessary for the promotion of thinking skills (see Chapter 7).

(c) In consequence also, it is very difficult to build in *progression,* as HMI found.

(d) A topic-web approach has also in the past masked the need for primary teachers to achieve some grasp of the procedures and frameworks of particular subjects, restricting their functioning to a *pre-disciplinary* level (Warwick, 1973), even at the upper junior end of the primary school.

To be coherent, however, does not mean that topic-work has to be inflexibly tied to subjects. It does mean that the teacher as curriculum planner has a basic awareness and understanding of the distinctive inputs subjects can make to the curriculum. These help to provide a coherent structure for nurturing thinking skills, and should be seen, as Chapters 1 and 2 suggest, as resources. There are three important criteria which need to be considered in producing coherent topic schemes. These are *balance, sequence and focus.*

Balance is vital from the preliminary stages of planning. It requires the achievement of some equilibrium between the subject inputs relevant to the topic of study. A lack of equilibrium may be merely the outcome of the biases of the people engaged in the planning. Thus, topics may be unbalanced because the teachers concerned know more about history than geography, or vice versa.

Sequence is particularly endangered by ill-focused topic schemes. Sequencing is important in its close association with ideas of progression. This involves matching work to the ability and experience of pupils at each phase of development. Sequence is easier to implement through units dedicated to the more linear skills of a particular element of a subject area, such as the map-reading skills of geography. The more complex the topic-web, the more difficult it is to do this, for it is virtually impossible to establish parallel sequences between diverse areas of study.

Focus also is lost if the perils of the more indiscriminate topic-webs are not appreciated. One way of establishing focus in topics which relate to geography is through *place-based* schemes. Thus local study, in which the themes introduced are focused on a particular locality, has long been one of the most successful approaches to topic work. The Geography Working Group has usefully revived the concept of the *locality study.* Primary teachers are finding localities a valuable focus for topic work, as small places offer a framework for an integrated approach, allowing both subject themes and cross-curricular elements to be permeated.

The other key element of focus is *conceptual*. This is based on the *distinctive* contributions of particular subjects like geography. A topic is not distinctively geographical just because it is about a particular place, however. It must relate also to the accepted procedures and concepts associated with the subject. As a brief check-list, a geography-focused topic will include

- locational knowledge;
- specific places;
- often a range of scales, from local to global;
- the use of maps and, especially for more distant places, photographs (for geography, like art, is essentially a visual subject);
- links between physical and human environments;
- enquiry-based approaches, including fieldwork in the local area and other places that can be visited;
- the promotion of caring attitudes towards the environment.

Establishing the Links

Part of the case for geography in the curriculum stems from its valuable *bridging role*. All places in history, for example, have had a geography. The links between physical geography and earth science are so close that they are hard for an outsider to distinguish. So for a start geography is a helpful bridge between the humanities and sciences. No self-respecting geographer also will deny her or his interest in the aesthetic appreciation of the landscape.

Let us here establish some coherent linkages for geography-focused topic work. For reasons emphasised later, this study will focus on the connections between three foundation subjects in the National Curriculum; *geography, history and art,* specifically in the context of *environmental education,* a cross-curricular theme. Because this chapter is a contribution to a book on geographical education, the topics covered will be geography-focused. But they could as easily and legitimately be history- or art-focused. Let us approach the principles of such linkage from pieces of evidence – first the non-geographical point of view, however.

The View from History

The History Working Group, like other subject groups, was asked by the Secretary of State to identify links with other areas of the curriculum. It pointed out that all history happened in place as well as time, and identified four benefits of closely-related curriculum planning in *history and geography.*

1 Both subjects benefit from each others' *methods of enquiry* involving:
   — investigation of human issues and values;
   — the interpretation of evidence;
   — the promotion of the skill of seeing things through other people'-
     points of view (*empathy*), with those in the past in the case of
     history, and with those in distant places in the present in the case of
     geography.

2 *Mapping skills* are of use to pupils in their study of history.

3 The two subjects *share themes* such as transport, industry, agriculture,
   settlement and population, to which each brings its own distinctive
   approaches.

4 All patterns and issues of concern to geographers have their *roots in
   history,* while an understanding of history is enhanced by knowledge
   about geographical context. This mutual relationship is especially
   evident in *local studies.*

The History Working Group was briefer but equally to the point over
links with art and the arts in general. It stressed that the arts offered a
rich and incomparable range of primary sources for the study of history,
including firm evidence and also subtle clues to how people felt in the
past.

The View from Art

Meanwhile, which subject working group submitted the following statements of attainment?

   — Make annotated diagrams/maps to show the journey from home to
     school and important personal landmarks on the journey.
   — Identify interesting details in the local area.
   — Work in groups to make a photomontage of focal points in the
     community: for example, the local market, the park and the super-
     market.

It was the Art Working Group, though could it not equally well have
been the Geography?

Such natural links are of course no new discovery, though they have
long been neglected. In 1982 the Schools Council published the recommendations of its project, *Art and the Built Environment,* which was
particularly interesting in its outline of the complementary of subjects in
relation to environmental education. Among the benefits of art education it listed:

- a more demanding, detailed and analytical approach to observation and recording of features of the built environment;
- focus on the aesthetic and design aspects of the built environment;
- promotion of critical skills in appraising that environment;
- development of personal responses to it.

The report acknowledged that other subjects, such as geography, had relevant roles to play in environmental education, but no one subject was more important than another, and by themselves each could only offer a partial understanding. They should be viewed as complementary and mutually supportive. The equation of environmental education with geography, history and science was criticised as over-stressing the collection and recording of factual information, and the importance of measurement and objective recording and classification. Art education helped to move beyond the factual survey and mental exercise to a more qualitative appraisal and interpretation, bringing in personal feelings and reactions: what has been termed 'getting behind the curtains' of the built environment. Art education thus complements geography and history in focusing on:

- redressing the neglect of aesthetic/emotional responses;
- promoting attention to visual discrimination – the 'artist's eye';
- promoting an architect's appreciation of the built environment and landscape design;
- fostering a sense of place;
- fostering an awareness of roots;
- promoting skills of drawing, field sketching, and landscape photography, leading to high quality displays of material.

A vital component in the cultivation of these skills is the use of *fieldwork*. To the idea of the town or country trail is added that of the *sensory walk*. In addition to the questions of the geographer and historian can be added those of the art specialist.

— Where did you go?
— What did you see? (Answer as sketch or picture.)
— What did you hear?
— What did you smell?
— What did you taste?
— What did you feel?
— What words did you come across?
— What were you reminded of?
— What thoughts did you have?

Similarly the Schools Council's *Art and Craft Education 8–13 Project* (1974) reinforced the point that the graphic arts fostered the skills of recording in a visual form that was often more revealing than pages of written description, and helped to sharpen observation and promote visual awareness in a unique way. The close links between the skills developed through integrated fieldwork in art and geography in developing aesthetic appreciation of the environment and a sense of place are arguably as important as the obvious links between geography and history, and geography and science.

The View from Environmental Education

As already noted, many of the links between the three subjects occur in the context of the environment. The National Curriculum Council's *Curriculum Guidance* document No. 7, *Environmental Education* (1990) reinforces the widely accepted view that there are three aspects to environmental education:

• Education *in* or *through* the environment, referring to fieldwork and enquiry-based education in general.
• Education *about* the environment, that is, gaining a basic knowledge and understanding of the environment.
• Education *for* the environment, which involves the ability to make informed choices and judgements on environmental issues; to find ways of caring for the environment; to find solutions to environmental problems; and to foster constructive attitudes towards the environment. (pp.10–12)

The HMI *Environmental Education 5–16* document in the *Curriculum Matters series* (1989) outlined the contribution of our three subjects to environmental education as follows:

Geography

— Mapping skills
— Field study skills
— Use of aerial and ground photographs and satellite imaging
— Investigation of physical and human conditions
— Grasp of local, national and global scales of activity.

History

— A sense of time and chronology
— A sense of continuity and change
— Use and respect for evidence

— Understanding the historical development of the environment.

Art

— Awareness and appraisal of the environment: its aesthetic qualities
— The concepts of design as it affects the environment (p.16).

The Curriculum Council for Wales delineation of the contribution of different subject contributions to *Environmental Education* in its advisory document on this cross-curricular theme (1992) highlighted, among other things, the importance of art education (p.10) and, in an associated poster on this cross-curricular theme, outlined the nature of this contribution as follows:

'Art education helps pupils develop a critical awareness of their environment and encourages a personal and sensitive response to their surroundings. The environment also provides a rich source of study and stimulus for a variety of art, craft and design work.'

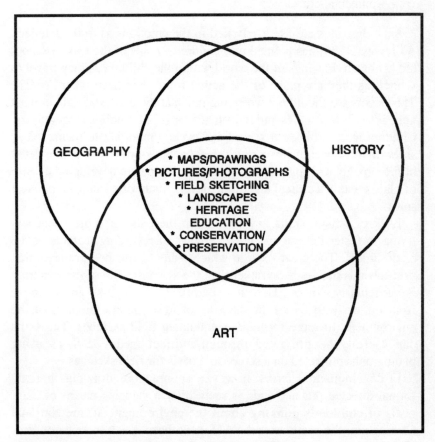

Figure 9.1: Linking geography, history and art

Figure 9.1 summarises key elements in the overlap between geography, history and art.

Approaches through Skills Development

For some time geography educationists have been interested in the links between the development of children's drawing and map-making skills. There is a clear development sequence from children's early spontaneous drawings of their environment, to increasingly tutored picture maps, plans and, finally, formal maps. The development of these skills is closely related to environmental experience. Brittain (1979) has noted that:

> 'Past studies have paid little attention to the development of art forms up to the age of six. However, there is a clear development progression. A good deal of the emphasis (should be)...on the potential for creative behaviour as a natural means of a child's organising and using environmental stimuli.' (p.vi)

Such drawings are as closely tied to the emotions as to the intellect. As Joicey (1986) has pointed out, children's maps of the way to school are 'as much drawings of the world within the children as they travel to school, as they are plans of the actual route they have taken' (p.95). This is why we should not worry too much at the early stage about what appear as inaccuracies judged on the basis of Euclidean geometry. Children tend to pick out scenes and events important to them. Joicey shrewdly observed that as a result they become aware of 'the fine detail of the small place' (p.6) and thus start the journey to developing a sense of places that is a critical test of the development of a true geographical spirit.

Lack of artistic skills has often been the bane of subject teachers trying to foster diverse and creative ways of recording features of the environment. The creative urge which leads to finished products that veer towards the aesthetic rather than the scientific end of the spectrum is particularly evident. Here it is helpful to distinguish and to move from the early focus on the drawing of idiosyncratic pictures of the environment, to more formalised annotated field sketches. The skills can usefully be promoted through indirect means such as using photographs projected on a screen as a basis for field sketches.

In developmental terms, however, spontaneous drawings predate formal directed practice and, as such, offer a valuable means of diagnosis of children's thinking about the environment. In the National Curriculum, the producers of SATS have been quick to seize on this. Thus in history young children at Key Stage 1 are asked to sequence in

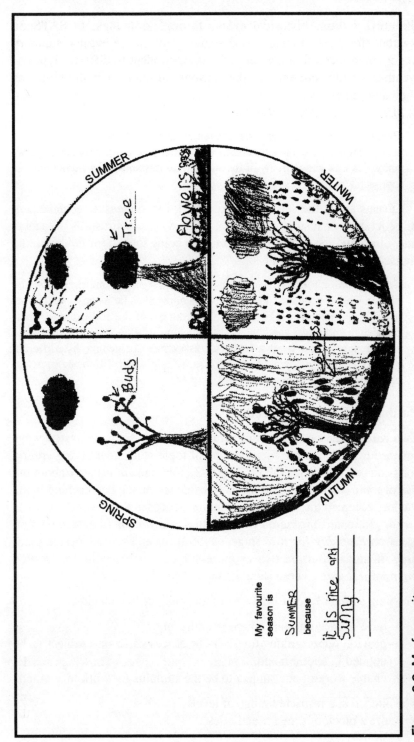

Figure 9.2: My favourite season

the correct order historical events through drawings. In SATS on weather (for some strange reason statutory in science but non-statutory in geography) children are similarly asked to identify different types of weather, or the sequence of the seasons, through their drawings, as shown in Figure 9.2.

SEAC have argued (1993) that:

'Pictorial and diagrammatic representation is often the simplest means for young children to demonstrate their knowledge and understanding of geography. For this reason many of the standard assessment tasks encourage this approach.' (p.13)

Caveats are at the same time expressed, for to measure achievement in geography or history should not depend on artistic skills. Teachers may often find the simple understandings being looked for hidden in the 'noise' of extraneous detail.

'Some children's drawings may not always be easily interpreted by the teacher. Children should, therefore, be encouraged as far as possible to label or annotate their drawings. If...still not certain...of the full extent of their knowledge and understanding...question them further orally...The quality of the drawings is not itself a focus for assessment of geography...different qualities of drawing...would not necessarily imply any difference in actual attainment in geography at that level...' (p.14)

Putting the Links into Practice

Two recent surveys of current primary practice have suggested ways forward towards a more focused type of topic work, identifying criteria for good practice. Thus OFSTED (1993), while unenthusiastic about the use of topic work, and wanting more evidence of subject teaching, none the less accepted the legitimacy of subject-focused topic work.

The National Curriculum Council, in a trial version of a document on ideas on *Planning for Key Stage 2* (1992), meanwhile advocated planning of units based on two or more subject orders, which it entitled *inter-subject units*. These should, claimed NCC,

• contain aspects taken from two or more subjects which either

— have some common content or skills; or,
— provide opportunities for skills or processes in one subject to be applied in another; and,
— enable work in one subject to be the stimulus for work in another;

• be pitched at a restricted range of levels;
• require a block of time for activities.

This suggested an officially approved compromise between strict subject work and over-expansive topic work, except that the terminology of the 'inter-subject unit' must have been regarded officially as suspect and did not emerge in the final version of the document. In its trial version, geography and art were linked in a case study exploring the recording of observations through fieldwork, with the relevant complementary Statements of Attainment from both subject orders helpfully identified, and the links justified.

> 'In observing the local area and its use for work and leisure (geography Order), there are opportunities for pupils to practise and develop the skills of investigating and recording images firsthand (art Order). Sketches and notes made can be the basis for further work and will meet the requirements of the geography Order which require pupils to represent real or imaginary places. Pupils can develop further their skills of analysis in comparing the different purposes of art using sources, for example maps, signs, photographic sketches, models, paintings, etc. and extending subject-specific vocabulary relevant to both subjects, for example, landscape, sketching, symbols.' (p.23)

Focused Topic Work: Combining Geography, History and Art

There are at least three levels at which geography, history, art and, inevitably, environmental education, are naturally connected.

1 At the *skills* level, there are links between:

— children's early drawings and map-making;
— pictures of landscapes and field sketches;
— interpretation of landscape drawings and paintings and photographs.

2 *Landscape appreciation,* whether rural or urban, is closely attached to the promotion of the basic values of environmental education. Before children are likely to want to care for the environment, they must learn to communicate about it and appreciate it.

3 *Heritage education,* which in content terms is the branch of environmental education most naturally bringing together geography, history and art, encompasses:

— museum and gallery visits;
— field work on vernacular (domestic) architecture;
— archaeology and industrial archaeology site visits;
— visits to famous historic buildings;
— conservation/preservation issues;

— at the broader scale, studies through indirect observation and enquiry-based learning of similar topics in distant places.

Case Studies

Direct Study: Fieldwork and Vernacular Architecture

Many primary schools are to be found in old villages and Victorian suburbs. In linking geography, history and art, it has already been noted that fieldwork in the form of a *town or village trail* is an invaluable means of integration. Similarly, ideas on appraising local vernacular architecture and other aspects of the urban environment were identified some time ago by Ward and Fyson, members of the Town and Country Planning Association, in their *Streetwork* (1973). These have subsequently been picked up by the English Heritage organisation, which similarly has offered useful advice to schools, in identifying, for example, how the heritage work it promotes can be supported from different subjects and cross-curricular areas of the National Curriculum. Other useful ideas on integrating these subject areas in town trails have been offered by Jex (1979), Howard (1979), and Rudd (1980).

To these could be added the more subjective questions identified above in helping to 'get behind the curtains' of the townscape. For example, children could be asked to seek out two or three different viewpoints and produce drawings of what they observe, together with descriptive responses as to how they feel about what they observe. They could also identify through labelled drawings individual buildings of different styles and the nature of the spaces around them, and offer judgements on whether they contribute favourably to the environment or not. As part of the art work, children could be asked to take their own photographs of the urban landscape for a photomontage, to be linked with other presentations for which they were responsible. In terms of social history, for an old school, log books, admissions registers and punishment books could offer, as they did in this Victorian suburb, supportive detail, bringing to life the experiences and feelings of some of the people who inhabited the area in late Victorian times. In these ways a conception of the 'fine detail of the small place' can be built-up as a basis for informed comment on the current quality of the environment and how it can be improved or worsened.

Indirect Study: Historic Defensive and Heritage Site

A long-standing but still useful approach to cross-curricular study is the *concentric* framework (see, for example, Masterton, 1969) in which, starting with a series of local localities, direct study observation of the home environment is followed by potentially equally 'living' (see Chapter 5) indirect studies of distant places. In linking geography with art and history a particularly useful theme is that of the ancient defensive site which often later became and remains a heritage location – a magnet for tourists. Such locations are plentiful in Britain, and also in distant places. Thus a locality study of Corfe, Conwy or Edinburgh castles can be a prelude to an overseas locality study, in this case a famous location in Greece.

Figure 9.3 suggests how a great historic building, say the Parthenon, and the ancient defensive site on which it stands, the Acropolis in Athens (9.4), can be studied through history, art and geography, meeting various requirements of the Programmes of Study in the three subjects, including the history Core Study Unit on Ancient Greece (see also Nicholson, 1991). Such material illustrates that even within the confines of a National Curriculum, natural cross-curricular links can readily be found and implemented.

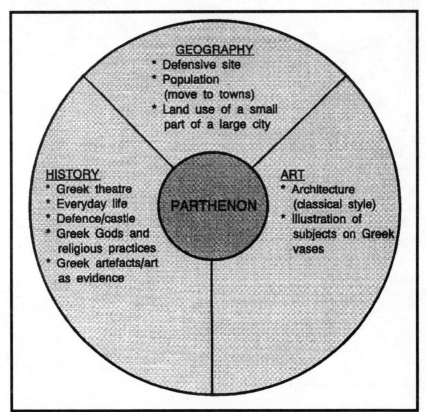

Figure 9.3: The Parthenon: Linking geography, history and art

Figure 9.4: The Acropolis: Defensive site

Address

English Heritage Education Service, Keysign House, 429 Oxford Street, London W1R 2HD.

CHAPTER 10

Linking Geography with Mathematics and Science: Curriculum Integration in a Primary School (Enquiry-based Geographical Study)

John Kenyon

Introduction

Happily it was a sunny day during the class field trip to study a river. One of the pupils, Peter, had managed to fill one of his wellington boots with water but that was not important as in his 'river dip' net he had caught a stickleback and, even more exciting, he had observed that the fish was pregnant. Peter gathered a group of interested young field-workers as he expounded his knowledge about pregnant fish. He looked sideways at the teacher saying rhetorically that sticklebacks 'lay' their eggs in a nest. The teacher could neither disagree or agree. There would need to be research into some textbooks back at school to arrive at a definitive answer. Peter was not the most conscientious of pupils. He was often hard to stimulate. The fieldwork trip about the river appeared to be as exciting and interesting to him as it seemed to be to the rest of the class. It was ostensibly a geography trip but skills and areas of knowledge were touching other areas of the National Curriculum. Pupils were also deviating from prescribed tasks as they made 'important' discoveries that were not necessarily the focus of the fieldwork study. In the view of the teacher in charge of the group of pupils, this was a very positive development as the hope and expectation had been to provide an opportunity for the children to engage in some open-ended activities as well as completing set tasks.

The main emphasis behind the organisation of the fieldwork study had been to integrate the subject areas of maths, science and geography, and the field trip was the culmination of careful planning where children had been helped progressively to develop their skills of enquiry, using the school environment.

The field trip had been organised to address one of the major issues that has developed in primary education since the implementation of the National Curriculum, that of perceived overload of curriculum content. It was an attempt to explore an approach to teaching that focuses on the learner whilst delivering progressive learning *within subject areas,* the contention being that much overload can often be attributed to the way the curriculum is organised. The National Curriculum is structured in subjects but it does not necessarily follow that it needs to be delivered in a subject format to pupils. Indeed, teaching that is narrowly subject-specific will not take advantage of the many natural relationships in knowledge, skills and understanding that co-exist between the many subject areas. These relationships are especially useful for the early stages of learning.

Teachers of young children find that pupils, if allowed, do not restrict their learning to the narrow confinement of subject areas but will follow their curiosity initially in an unsystematic manner, rather like Peter, which invariably leads them across the boundaries of subject areas. It is one of the teacher's functions to introduce structure into the pupils' learning.

The Curriculum Structure

If there is to be structure in an integrated approach, it is necessary that teachers have some understanding of the subject areas they teach and it is important that this understanding includes some form of progressive framework and notions of assessment criteria.

Subjects in the curriculum are of human creation, a convenient means of categorising forms of knowledge and skills. The boundaries between these subjects are not watertight. Many subjects are related or have areas of learning in common. This is especially true with the relationships that exist between geography, mathematics and science.

The connections between geography and the two subjects and their sub-divisions are particularly wide ranging:

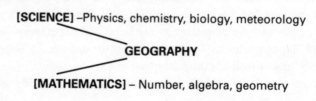

[SCIENCE] –Physics, chemistry, biology, meteorology

GEOGRAPHY

[MATHEMATICS] – Number, algebra, geometry

These subjects are also related in the way that a great deal of learning needs to take place through activity, i.e. that is enquiry-based, and requires some form of practical application to enable pupils to acquire skills. It is through activity that pupils can display learning that can be assessed and as well as this develop the important areas of language and numeracy that are essential to promote learning in *all* areas of the curriculum.

The Inter-Subject Enquiry-Based Approach

Assessment Issues

It needs to be recognised that even in the context of state-prescribed assessment not everything a pupil does has to be assessed and recorded. To a large degree, the finished product or piece of work presented by a pupil can be evidence for a great deal of cross-disciplinary achievement. The finished product of work is the summative evidence. The child's ongoing work will be subjected to formative assessments as the teacher interacts with the pupil. Too much emphasis on recording these formative assessments can contribute to the perceived overload of the curriculum. This point was accepted by the Dearing Interim Report in July 1993.

> 'But teachers have found that the degree of detail and prescription intrudes into the proper exercise of professional judgement and tends to diminish the quality of educational experience they can offer.' (para 3.9)

> 'Despite the fact that there is no legal requirement to record achievement in relation to the many prescribed statements of attainment, many teachers have tried scrupulously to do just this. This has proved to be a heavy administrative burden.' (para 3.10)

Inter-subject Enquiry

To embark on an integrated cross-disciplinary approach to learning requires the teacher to be precise about how he or she defines 'integrated approach'. Decisions need to be made regarding the degree of structure to a pupil's learning that is to be directed by the teacher and how far there will be a possibility for pupils to engage in open-ended activities which will overlap into different curriculum areas.

The National Curriculum is subject-oriented and is an entitlement curriculum. There is a legal obligation placed upon teachers to deliver education in certain prescribed areas. The method the teacher may choose to deliver the National Curriculum is, however, not prescribed and the recent movement away from an emphasis on continuous assessment based upon Statements of Attainment can release the teacher from a strait-jacket of subject-specific continuous assessment to one concentrating on the relationships of learning objectives between different subject areas. It is important, however, that the teacher maintains a structure to learning that recognises the progression of learning, individual to subject areas. Pupils need to know about and identify the skills and areas of knowledge contained within different curriculum areas because subject areas are the means by which we learn to classify and synthesise information. To develop an approach that does not progressively teach a child the skills and individual approaches unique to subject areas would be a disservice.

The reality of practical teaching requires pupils to have some structure and the teacher must be active in guiding learning within this structure if the learning is going to be progressive. Subject areas can permeate an integrated thematic topic but they have to be relevant to it and be progressive not only within the theme itself but within the individual subject's own terms of reference.

Merely choosing a theme and clustering subject-specific activities around the theme is not a progressive approach even when Attainment Target numbers can be attached! The approach has to be more sophisticated. Activities based around the theme need to be inter-subject oriented but planning must include the development of subject-specific skills and knowledge prior to integration. The specific subject skills can be then applied within an integrated theme. In this way the pupils develop cross-curricular skills and can develop learning within different subject areas during a single activity. This need not be as complex as it sounds because there exist many naturally 'integratable' subject areas especially suited to the early stages of learning.

The approach that can synthesise the various subject areas could best be described as enquiry-based inter-subject studies.

Case Studies

Main Topic – Study a Place

Sub-topics – (1) Our School
(2) A River Study

Introduction

The topic was carried out with a class of Year 5 pupils. Geographical themes were chosen and both the mathematical and scientific elements of enquiry were integrated into them. It was important to ensure that the areas of learning in the individual subject areas were developed sufficiently for pupils to operate effectively on the practical enquiry elements within the sub-topics. The first sub-topic required a greater emphasis on developing the skills for the 'practical application of mathematics'. Science became more dominant in the second sub-topic.

The 'Our School' theme was designed to develop practical skills of gathering information about a place. The school seemed the best initial topic to study as it was an environment that had been known to the children for a number of years. The children were initially required to produce sketch maps and draw rough diagrammatic representations of observed areas within the school grounds – the development would be to use these sketches as the basis to produce more mathematically accurate representation.

The main emphasis placed on the pupils' work was on producing diagrammatic representation on a two-dimensional plane and also developing an understanding of ways to communicate direction. The children were required to work cooperatively in groups and the groups contributed to the final product which was to be a map and/or plan of the school.

Progression from the first theme to the second, 'A River Study', was to utilise and develop skills in the first themes within an environment not known by the pupils. The area of study chosen was the source of the River Bollin in Macclesfield Forest. The mathematical and mapping skills could be developed and scientific method could be used to gain greater knowledge and understanding of the area.

Assessment could be made during work in both themes but this was more formative in nature as the teacher attempted to develop skills and knowledge in order to enable pupils to work independently during fieldwork. The summative assessments were to be found in the finished products produced by the pupils. Planning was thus primarily geared to enable pupils to undertake an enquiry, rather than to any specific attainment targets. National Curriculum ATs could be recorded at the summative assessment stage.

Planning was also an important element in organising the cross-curricular nature of the enquiry as it was essential only to integrate areas of learning that were relevant to the aim of the topic. To attempt to over-integrate the topic would lose its focus.

The work pupils carried out needed to be communicated or recorded in some form and thus the English element also has an important part to play, though this will not be emphasised in this chapter.

The topic needed to have specific aims and objectives.

Aims

— To work cooperatively in groups.
— Use various skills to gain a better understanding of place.
— Develop cross-curricular enquiry techniques.

Objectives

Geography

— Draw accurate sketch maps
— Draw plans to scale
— Use symbolic representation
— Develop map reading skills – read route maps, read O.S. maps, six-figure references, understand contours, measure distance using scale on maps, use maps to make cross sections, read road maps, use map symbols
— Use Silva compass
— Gain information about rivers using secondary sources
— Learn about occupations within a locality
— Become aware of the problem of water pollution.

Mathematics

— Measure using different types of apparatus, i.e. trundle wheel, tape measure, metre stick
— Construction of triangles
— Drawing to scale
— Measure in angles
— Reinforcement of number bonds
— Measuring temperature.

Science

— Properties of insulation to discover what influences fluctuation in temperature
— Floating and sinking – analyse different materials in water
— Movement
— Magnetism.

Science skills were to be of paramount importance and pupil work on science was designed to develop skills which, although classified as science, have significant application in geographical enquiry. The prac-

Scientific Investigative Skills

Scientific process skills developed for geographical investigations

Observing	Discussing	Raising Questions
Using appropriate senses with appropriate accuracy	Able to discuss work carried out Able to clarify ideas from discussion	Able to raise questions that can be investigated Raise questions based upon own investigations
Sorting and grouping Able to identify and sort materials and physical features to own criteria Noticing differences Noticing similarities	**Expressing and testing ideas** Able to test out ideas in an unsystematic way	**Noticing change** Able to explain what has changed
Classifying Able to sort to logical criteria, e.g. mass vertebrate/invertebrate geographical features,etc	**Planning an investigation** Able to proffer hypothesis – predict results from hypothesis and is testable Systematic approach to investigation	**Investigating change** Finding more about change
	Problem-solving Ability to apply skills, knowledge and understanding to a problem for which there is no obvious answer Able to plan out investigation, evaluate information, revise action, draw conclusions, report findings	**Explain change** Able to formulate ideas as to the causation of change and exhibits capability of testing hypothesis

Figure 10.1

tical difficulty with learning to use skills from a geographical standpoint is that much time on actual fieldwork enquiry can be lost whilst teaching basic skills on site. It is more cost-effective if the basic skills are developed in the classroom or school area first. Hence, for this projected topic, a great deal of science work was planned that related to tasks to be carried out by the pupils during their geographical fieldwork based on the River Bollin.

Skills developed were – observation, discussion, raising questions, expressing and testing ideas, planning an investigation, problem-solving, sorting and grouping, noticing change, explaining change. (See Figure 10.1)

1. The School

The first stage was for the pupils to be helped to develop a concept of the school as a 'locality' which required them to become aware of all the various areas not normally within the children's domain. The care-taker's room, kitchen storage areas, etc. The children also needed to look at side elevations of the school to learn to observe the materials used. (See Figure 10.2)

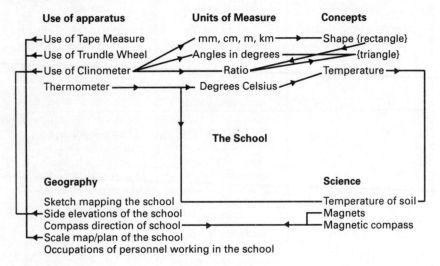

Figure 10.2

The first part of the work was to draw and sketch aspects of the school. The children were allowed the freedom to sketch and draw different aspects of the school and whilst this happened the teacher interacted and spoke to the children about the size and dimensions of the school. Pupils were allowed to colour their sketches.

There was a great deal of information acquired by pupils through general discussion. Interestingly, such features as there being four classes on one side of the school whilst only three on the other were discovered for the first time! There were other important discoveries such as the large water tower at the front of the school. Questions regarding its purpose were asked and this led to a number of openings for learning regarding cybernetic systems as well as water flows. It was certainly a revelation to realise how much of the actual school had been 'unobserved' by many of the pupils.

The children became aware of the number of people employed at the school and the wide variety of occupations necessary for its efficient running. Interestingly, the children did find it hard to see what the function of a headteacher was when not teaching!

The development of key mathematical skills was essential. Accurate measuring and the concept of area needed to be reinforced. Work on measurement needed to be coordinated between individuals and groups and it was thus essential that everyone could work to the same degree of accuracy. Each group measured the hall and the length of the main corridor using tape measures and trundle wheels and results were compared. Checking of results was carried out until there was a consensus of the parameters of accuracy.

Groups were then required to measure different areas of the school and make an accurate scale plan. The children at this time could choose their own scale. The groups needed to coordinate this work to ensure that there were no duplications. Interestingly the children discovered that many areas of the school they thought would be easily mapped proved to be the most difficult. The main corridor has cloakroom bays off it and these bays are not set off the corridor at right angles. The children eventually developed a number of strategies to measure the angle of a corner of a wall ranging from cutting out paper corners to using sticks of two metres. Later, consensus of scale was required for the whole school plan.

Side elevations of the school were required. This involved the use of the clinometer. The method used was to move a measured distance from the item to be measured, take an angle reading with the clinometer one metre above ground level (using a metre stick). This required mathematical preparation and the children were engaged in activities that required measuring angles, constructing triangles and practice using the clinometer. The children were then required to produce their own sheet with instructions about how to measure the height of objects using a clinometer. (This angle work was also an important basis for future work developing the skill to use a Silva compass.) Having carried out

all this mathematical 'groundwork' there was then the need to standardise everything in order to develop the plan.

Each group produced a standard scale representation of the areas of
the school they had measured and theoretically the whole thing fitted
together like a jigsaw: which it did to an acceptable degree of accuracy.
The finished map or plan needed information on it and the pupils
decided to use symbols and colour to indicate areas of the school and a
key to the school map was produced.

Activities carried out in parallel with the map work was to gain more
scientific information about the school. Readings were taken to ascer-
tain the temperature of the soil in various places and also analysis of the
type of soil around the school was made.

The children were also introduced to the Silva compass. The children
used special compasses developed at Liverpool University for primary
pupils (see Chapter 4). The initial work on the compass involved
looking at its properties, i.e. the magnetic element of the compass, and
also making the children aware that this type of compass has a 360
degree protractor built into it. Work on the compass at this stage was
limited to establishing the direction of various features of the school
from different standpoints. The more sophisticated use of the Silva
compass would be developed in the second theme.

2. Field Study

The field study of the River Bollin was planned to build on and extend
the skills previously learnt. The children were required to acquire
knowledge and understanding of an environment they had not visited
previously. The study was to concentrate on the source of a river. The
location chosen was in the Macclesfield Forest where there is a small
tributary of the River Bollin. Four points on the river were designated to
be studied. The points were chosen for the children because an initial
reconnoitre had established the areas to be safe. The study needed to
have a narrow focus in order that the children could utilise their developing skills to acquire data to gain geographical information about an
area (see Figure 10.3).

Geographical skills to be utilised

— Read map – to be able to envisage an environment from informa-
    tion on a map. The children studied O.S. maps of the area and
    then drew pictures of what they thought the area looked like.
— Route maps – work out a route map to Macclesfield Forest from
    the school.

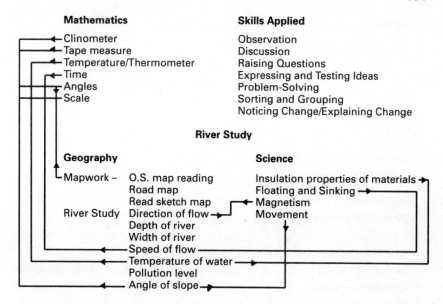

Figure 10.3

— Follow sketch maps – to use a sketch map to find way to the various designated points to be studied in Macclesfield Forest.

Science/Maths skills

— Scientific measurement to draw conclusions about an environment
— Temperature of stream/river
— Rate of flow
— Pollution level
— Dimensions
— Angle of slope.

In a one day field study, time is of the essence and it was important that children's activity concentrated on work that could only be carried out whilst on the location. It was important, therefore, for pupils to rehearse the activities in their groups prior to the visit.

Pre-Visit Activities

Children were grouped and each group worked on activities that provide the skills necessary for the visit.

Science

Temperature
Looking at properties of insulation. Measuring temperature of liquids

in different types of vessels over period of time.

Floating and Sinking
Finding materials that floated and were visible, e.g. balls, corks, matchsticks (corks were seen as the most appropriate article for the job in hand).

Movement
Work on the pendulum – timing the swings at different lengths and different masses. This was preparatory work for measuring the rate of flow of the water.

Magnetism
The effect of a magnet on a compass.
The effect of an electrical circuit on a magnet – the children observed how the needle of magnetic compass moved when placed within the proximity of an electrical circuit (models were built to demonstrate this phenomenon).
Investigating the properties of magnetism.

Mathematics

Measuring time using stop watches and timers.
Angles using Silva compass – i.e. standing at a point in the classroom then making an angle reading to points in the classroom. This work was then extended to the previous topic and angles related to the school plan were calculated. The children made 'buried treasure' maps on the school field. A starting point was designated and, using compass angles and length measuring, a map was constructed to find the pot of gold. Children had a great deal of fun trying out each other's treasure maps.

Geography

Map Work
Looking at different types of maps of area to be visited.
Road map to destination.
Large scale map – studying the contours and describing what the place will look like. Drawing what they think they will see.
Using measures to work out scale.
Analysing route map
Secondary sources: looking for information about rivers.

Visit Activities

On the actual trip pupils had to take readings from the points on the river. They had to:

- Indicate direction of flow using compass angles.
- Measure the width of the river using a tape measure.
- Measure the depth of the river (at the edge and in the middle) using a metre stick.
- Measure the speed of flow at a rate per metre. This was calculated by timing the length of time it took a cork to travel two metres and dividing the answer by two.
- Measure temperature using a thermometer.
- Measure slope. This was achieved by the same two pupils in each group standing a measured distance apart, one upstream and one downstream and a clinometer reading was taken.
- Identifying mini-beasts. The children were provided with a diagrammatic chart with pictures of the different types of animal life to be found in the river. Using nets the children dipped the stream and identified the animals from the chart.
- Quality of water. Using the animal chart it was possible to identify the types of animals that could not live in polluted water and those that could. The children could make a rough and ready assessment on the quality of water.

The children undertook their tasks with enthusiasm. The work carried out at school had enabled them to develop the ability to work cooperatively and the role of the adults was one of encouraging prediction, hypothesising and interpretation of results. No amount of preparation can foresee actual on-site problems. The first point of survey was a very small tributary of the Bollin, no more than a small trench approximately 10cm. wide. It was a difficult task to measure depth in three places and hard to find a stretch of water that would float a cork for a reasonable length in order to measure the rate of flow. Many of the children decided that some of the measurements were not possible and did what they could, and then moved to the next designated test site.

The test for pollution by identifying mini-beasts was extremely absorbing for many of the children and as it was the first time the children had been able to engage in activity of this type proved to be time-consuming owing to the interest it generated.

Observation of the children indicated that the activities prior to the visit enabled work to be focused upon the gathering and interpretation of data rather than elaborate explanations by teachers of the processes required to obtain relevant information.

Conclusion

The whole of the work carried out by this group of children had been designed to obtain maximum advantage from a day field trip. The activities prescribed by the teacher for the children to carry out were cross-curricular. Many of the interpretations from data obtained were geographical in nature.

The emphasis on skills and enquiry enabled hypotheses to be made that could be reinforced or discounted by research using secondary sources at school. Hypotheses such as rivers flow in a straight line down the side of a hill were proved to be false, as the compass readings of the direction of flow indicated changes of direction. It was discovered that the river did not flow fastest at the top of the hill – at its source – as many of the pupils had predicted. It speeded up further down stream when the river became wider. However, at the lowest point surveyed the flow was slower. The children were able to make generalisations about the character of flow of a typical river but appreciated that ideally further studies of different rivers in different places would be required to be sure about any assertion.

The river was found at first to be deepest in the middle, though one child waded into part of the river where there was a bend and found the deepest place to be at the inside of the bend. This led to a line of enquiry where the children observed silting and began to develop notions about what caused it and why silting occurred at particular points in a river. The questions and observations multiplied as the children found the application of their scientific, mathematical and geographical skills not only provided answers but raised further questions. The results of the data gathering activities were recorded and children's observations and recordings noted.

The finished work, as well as the field trip notes, could be used as a basis for National Curriculum summative assessments. The key point to be made is that the major orientation of the work was to the child's educational needs – which meant that activities were out of necessity cross-curricular as the children needed skills in a number of curriculum subjects to gain understanding about an environment or place.

The geographical elements of the studies, whilst important in their own right, enabled skills, in other curriculum areas to be utilised purposefully – the point being that the pupils were not encumbered with any requirement to restrict their enquiries to any individual curriculum subject owing to the fact that the teacher had planned pupil learning and activity progressively within each individual subject area.

In the event it was only young Peter who did not complete many of the prescribed tasks required by the teacher. He had been too happy observing his stickleback and other creatures he had caught. At school he went to the library and started to borrow books about fish, noting the names of different parts of their body and discovering the process by which fish are able to breathe under water. He proudly brought a book to show the teacher. It had an illustration of a stickleback laying eggs in a nest. 'See, I told you,' he said.

CHAPTER 11

'Read all about it': Using Children's Literature in Support of Primary Geography

Jeremy Krause

Introduction

'One day a girl heard about No Man's Land and immediately began to wonder where it was and who lived there.'
(From *The Clothes Horse and other Stories*, by Janet and Allan Ahlberg.)

Places and the environment have inspired equally all the creators of works of art, music and literature, whether or not the outcome is deemed to be successful. These creative people have been influenced by places and the environment and have responded in kind in the form of the written word and through all forms of artistic expression including art, music, dance and drama. Teachers make a similar use of place and environment to interest and encourage children to investigate and record and report on the world around them, as well as using the stimulus of the living world to be creative in their own right.

The use of literature in primary curriculum is put succinctly in the *Kingman Report:*

'...pupils are entitled to a reading curriculum which extends this understanding of the world and themselves, and which stimulates response. Consequently, such a curriculum needs to be varied and challenging, as do the reading and writing activities that stem from such reading'.

The use of literature is also recognised in *English for Ages 5–16* (NCC 1988):

'An active involvement with literature enables pupils to share the experience of others'.

This chapter explores the contribution which all forms of literature can make to the teaching and learning of geography in the primary curriculum and as such aims to show how suitable literature might be chosen for use in the classroom and some exemplification of its use, together with some approaches to the use of literature with adults.

The Use of Literature in the Primary Geography Curriculum

The contribution of literature to the primary geography curriculum may be summarised as follows:

1 Literature can provide children with a wide range of access to the lives of other people, both near and far, in the United Kingdom and in other countries, and in a range of environments. In particular, it can extend the curriculum in a manageable way beyond the relatively narrow requirements of the statutory Orders for National Curriculum geography.

2 Literature can provide materials which complement and extend the use of other resources in the curriculum such as textbooks, photopacks, and tourist leaflets.

3 Literature can be used to develop the skills of geographical enquiry, in particular the gathering and interpretation of evidence from text, pictures and photos, with map reading where applicable.

4 Literature can help the reader to see aspects of geography in the context of people's lives – it can enliven interest and encourage investigation into parts of the geography curriculum which in themselves do not necessarily motivate the learner.

5 Literature can inspire children to write their own prose and poetry, based on their experiences of places and environments.

6 Literature can support major parts of the curriculum, such as topics or themes, by ensuring a range of relevant and applicable books are available in the classroom and library.

7 Literature can be used in INSET to encourage teachers to talk about geography and in particular the geographical potential of many books which are available within their school.

For the purposes of this chapter, literature will include all forms of literature, both prose and poetry, from picture books in which there is little or no text to story books in which there are few or no illustrations. Some literature may be about imaginary places or environments, but even here there is often a geographic potential which may be explored. Indeed Scoffham and Jewson (1993) argue that fairy tales, legends and myths can be used to develop geographical principles in relation to location, processes and the development of mapwork skills from the development of mental images of places to the use of author's maps and diagrams.

The use of picture books is sometimes felt to be unsuitable for older children, and yet in a subject such as geography, surely there is a major role for pictures which conjure up a landscape in a single image, a view which can show complex interactions that many words of text would fail to describe. Elaine Moss (1985) notes that 'picture books make exciting demands on their readers in terms of visual and verbal texture, emotional depths, imaginative heights, empathy, sympathy, structure and style.' Most adults cannot fail to be moved and impressed by the stunning visual messages which some authors and their illustrators have achieved in children's literature. Poetry can target certain parts of a situation for comment and give a clarity of view with regard to complex issues. It is a powerful medium and is well suited to drawing the reader's attention to key points, as well as for the recording and reporting of events.

The majority of the books which are referred to in support of the text are children's literature. However, reference is made to other literature, as this can be used both by the children in the classroom and by teachers either singly, in small groups, or for whole staff INSET and other curriculum development activities.

Choosing and Reviewing Literature

Geography has always featured within the primary curriculum particularly through local study and investigations of other lands and environments. The National Curriculum for geography sought to formalise and extend their geographical experience so that there were some common elements for all children.

The construction of an acceptable National Curriculum framework for geography caused much debate in professional and political circles, but the published outcome as the Orders in 1991 was an attempt to reflect the main aspects of the subject. There was a somewhat artificial division into five Attainment Targets of skills, places and themes, which helped the non-specialist teacher, in particular, to analyse what makes up geography. The analysis which follows uses the post-Dearing divisions, and links where relevant to some of the key ideas and concepts in the subject.

Geographical skills

The use of geographical enquiry to structure learning is recognised in the Programme of Study although this was not reflected in the old Attainment Targets, which focused narrowly upon skills of map work and some aspects of fieldwork. The broader range of enquiry skills is used in the context of investigations into places and environments, their form and characteristics and how they came to be as they are now and might be in the future. The contribution of literature to this process is considerable as it encourages the reader to be analytical by perceiving what the writer or illustrator is trying to communicate. As the National Curriculum Council's document *English for Ages 5-16* puts it:

'They will encounter and come to understand a wide range of feelings and relationships by entering vicariously the world of others...'

Some examples of the use of geographical skills are demonstrated in the poem, *High on the Hill*, by Tom Wright.

High on the hill I can see it all,
the anthill men and the doll's house town,
the bowl of the sea and the trim toy ships.
Here only the trees at hand are tall.

High on the hill I can touch a cloud
or measure miles with my fingertips,
can hide a town with a palm turned down
and drown its noise when I speak aloud.

High on the hill it's all a joke
and I wonder why I bothered at all
with the clockwork cars and the anthill folk
that height and distance make so small.

What uses could this be put to in terms of the concept of scale, mapping, sketching and the use of oblique views, together with an image of another place?

Some stories are accompanied by maps, plans and diagrams, as in *Summer in Small Street*, by Geraldine Kay, and *The Journey Home*, by Joanne Findall, and in recent years there has been a rapid growth in adventure stories linked to puzzles which include maps, for example in *Journey to the Lost Temple* (1990), one of The Usborne Puzzle Adventures.

It is unlikely that skill development will be taught in a decontextualised way and it is considered to be good practice if skill development is undertaken in a context where the range of skills are applied in an investigation or enquiry into places and environments.

Knowledge and understanding of places

Here there is potentially an extensive contribution from literature. In addition to the development of knowledge and understanding of places, literature can help to explore geographical concepts such as

— a sense of place through the writer's image of a place;
— location – why is this place where it is?
— similarity and difference – how is this place the same or different from the reader's place or locality?
— how is this place changing and why?

Two examples from literature of the characteristics of places are:

'What's funny about Small Street is all the houses are the same and all the people are different.' *Summer in Small Street*, by Geraldine Kay.

And, *Our School*, by Gareth Owen.

I go to Weld Park Primary,
It's near the underpass
And five blocks past the Cemetery
And two roads past the Gas
Works with the big tower that smells so bad
me and me mates put our hankies over our
faces and pretend we're being attacked
by poison gas...

Creating images of places and environments is where picture books can come into their own. There are many examples but the following are exceptional in their visual impact:

Where the forest meets the sea, Jeannie Baker (1987).
Window, Jeannie Baker (1991).
The Prairie Alphabet, by Yvette Moore and Jo Bannatyne-Cugnet (1992).

Physical Geography

Many stories bring in references to the physical environment and by doing so can be linked to physical geography. Interestingly, some of the most powerful writing is in the form of poetry. Here, for example, is a part of a poem which is a description of an African tropical storm.

A Sudden Storm, by Pious Oleghe.
'The wind howls, the trees sway,
The loose house top sheets clatter and clang,
The open window shuts with a bang,
And the sky makes night of the day...'

The following poem describes the area around the Victoria Falls.

The Victoria Falls, by William Plomer.
'These are the Victoria Falls, whose noisy gushing
Attracts a noisy and a gushing crowd
Who rush from every country in the world to gape
At this cascade which is the usual shape.

Over the brink a lot of water slops
By force of gravity, and many a tourist stops
And stares to see a natural law fulfilled
And quantities of water that never stop being spilled...'

And then, the very powerful image of the violent and challenging environment on the South Australian coast.

'Storm Boy lived between the South Australian Coorong and the sea. His home was the long, long snout of sandhill and scrub that curves away south eastwards from the Murray Mouth. A wild strip it is, windswept and tussocky with the flat shallow water of the Coorong on one side and the endless slam of the Southern Ocean on the other. They call it the Ninety Mile Beach. For thousands of miles around the cold, wet underbelly of the world the waves come sweeping in towards the shore and pitch down in a terrible ruin of white water and spray.' *Storm Boy*, by Colin Thiele.

Or, the description by the wildlife and landscape painter C. F. T. Tunnicliffe of the area south east of Macclesfield, Cheshire.

'To the right of the church, Ridge Hill began, a long hill which was one of the fingers of real wild country to the east. The road along its crest led into the heart of the wildest parts of east Cheshire, and on into Derbyshire, land of hills without end...The prospect westward was immense, for in that direction the Cheshire Plain stretched for fifty miles until it was stopped by the first hill outposts of Wales.' *My Country Book*, by C. F. Tunnicliffe.

A succinct and bleak account of a beach puts the mundanity of physical geography into a dramatic context.

A Beach of Stones, by Kevin Crossley-Holland.
'That stadium of roaring stones,
The suffering, O they are not dumb things,
Though bleached and worn when water
Strikes at them. Stones will be the last ones;
They are earth's bones, no easy prey
For breakers, and they are not broken
But diminish only, under the pestle,
Under protest. They shift through centuries,
Grinding their way towards silence.'

Or for young children.

Summerwords, by Ann and Roger Bonner.
'Sun high
sea wide
sand soft
low tide...'

Books about the weather and seasons abound and are readily available in most schools. Good examples are:
Our House on the Hill, Phillippe Dupasquier (1987): Same view point of the houses but shown through the seasons.
Lucy's Year, by Stephen Weatherill (1990).
and, *Garden in the City*, by Gerda Muller (1988).

Human Geography

The characteristics of human activity feature widely in literature since most stories and poems are about humans, their thoughts, ideas and activities. There are many stories which are set in towns or villages. There is an inevitable bias towards books about life in white middle class areas although books such as *Crossroads*, by Rachel Isadora, do give an insight into shanty towns in South Africa, home for migrant workers and their families. When it comes to industry there are some books about farms, but almost none about manufacturing industry, and our literature record here tends to rely still on the works of Victorians such as Charles Dickens or Arnold Bennett.

Many stories feature journeys and by doing so explore the concept of routeways – paths along which people and goods move. Some examples include: *My side of the mountain*, by Jean George, about a boy who runs away from his crowded New York home to the wildscape of the Catskill Mountains; or, *The Children on the Oregon Trail*, by A. Rutgers van der Loeff, which is about a journey made through the Cascade Mountains in the 1840s.

There are some very matter of fact books such as *The Railway Station*, by Phillippe Dupasquier, which is about everyday transport, or poems such as *Motor Cars*, by Rowena Bastin Bennett, which explores the curious behaviour of the rush hour.

Motor Cars
'From city window way up high,
I like to watch the cars go by.
They look like burnished beetles, black,
That leave a little muddy track
Behind them as they slowly crawl.

Sometimes they do not move at all
But huddle close with hum and drone
As though they feared to be alone.
They grope their way through fog and night
With the golden feelers of their light.'

Environmental Geography

The nature of the human and physical environments, and issues concerning conservation, feature a great deal in children's literature. These themes reflect increased awareness and concern about the planet as we move towards the end of the twentieth century. Central to this is the concept of the environment as being a single, complex highly interactive system.

Some writers have been particularly successful in bringing the concept into the form and structure of children's literature. A particularly stunning example is *One World*, by Michael Foreman. The book is about two children exploring the life on a rocky shoreline and how they create their own 'world' in a bucket from the contents of a rock pool.

'All the long afternoon they tended their tiny world. They added more seaweed shells and three more fish, but the more they added to their world, the more they took from the real world. The only things now floating in the pool were the feathers and the blob of oil.'

Some books are a real cry from the heart. In this category is *Antarctica*, by Helen Cowcher, where she shows in a brilliantly illustrated book how the wildlife of Antarctica is becoming increasingly threatened by people and their exploitation of this fragile environment.

'The penguins and the seals have always shared their world with ancient enemies, the Skuas and Leopard seals. But these new arrivals seem more dangerous. The seals and the penguins cannot tell yet whether they will share or destroy their beautiful Antarctica...'

The environmental theme is reflected in many poems and part of *Atmosfear*, by Sean O'Huigin, demonstrates this very clearly.

'...but bit by bit
and drop by drop
as humans make the
air grow hot
pumping garbage
and pollution...'

Small scale, but important changes in a locality are explored in *Trees*

Rule OK, by Sue Limb, where the author explores the serious issues of the removal of a tree from a suburban avenue in an amusing and effective way which could be used with children to help highlight environmental change in their locality.

Some books are hard to categorise, fortunately, in national curriculum terms, and are just exciting and interesting ways to explore the world. An example is *No Man's Land*, from *The Clothes Horse and other Stories*, by Janet and Allan Ahlberg.

> 'There are all kind of lands, as you know. There's Basutoland where the Basutos live; Scotland where the Scots live, and Heligoland where the Heligos live (or maybe go to). There's the Land where the Bong Tree grows, and the Happy land, far far away. There's Cloud Cookoo Land. There's the land flowing with Milk and Honey (and Rice Krispies too I hope). And...there's No Man's Land.'

Some words of caution!

The vast majority of children's literature was never written to meet the needs of the geography curriculum; the authors intended that their books should first, engage the reader and second, enable them to appreciate and understand things about people, their lives and the environment in which they live. Only occasionally are the books structured in a way which supports the systematic learning of geography either in the broad sense or in a reduced form as the National Curriculum for geography. The key issue for the teacher is to assess how to emphasise the characteristics which are geographical without detracting either from the broader educational message or the enjoyment of the reader.

The range of literature available to the reader will inevitably be affected by the availability of published books and the purchasing policy of the school or the local library. The geography curriculum does not include, as mentioned above, teaching and learning about places and environments beyond the U.K., in the developing world and in the European Community. The availability of books written in English about these places is likely to be restricted in form and whilst there will be many from the English speaking world which includes the Commonwealth and the United States there are likely to be very few translated from the French, Spanish and Chinese. This is not to imply that children should not become aware of other languages and cultures; it is that they will be more difficult to use purely for the geography curriculum.

Another related issue is the availability of books which reflect the rich multicultural society which is the U.K. in the latter part of the twentieth century. Many books still focus upon life in a white society. For example the *Katie Morag* stories by Mairi Hedderwick which are about Katie's life in the Outer Hebrides, are excellent in their own right and are certainly an engaging way of learning about another locality, but need to be counterbalanced by books such as *Babylon* by Jill Paton Walsh. At one level this story is about children exploring their locality and at another is about multi-ethnic British society with the use of Caribbean patois and reference to the migration of the children's family from Jamaica where two of the three children were born. These aspects, if handled in an informed manner, can contribute greatly to the richness of the curriculum.

The same can be true in some of the parts of the world greatly affected by immigration from Britain, such as Australia and Canada. It is only in recent years that books about the life and culture of the indigenous peoples of the so called 'first nations', such as the Aborigines and the North American Indians have become readily available. Examples include *Mother and daughter: the story of Daisy and Gladys Corunna* by Sally Morgan, which is about the enslavement by white Australians of aborigines on farmsteads in Australia. The author reflects upon the future:

'I like to think that no matter what we become, our spiritual tie with the land and the other unique qualities we possess will somehow weave their way through to future generations of Australians. This is our land, after all; surely we've got something to offer.'

One particularly poor example of an ill-informed way of investigating other societies and cultures is *A Country Far Away* by Phillippe Dupasquier, which uses the good idea of running a split page system to focus on two places at once, one in the U.K. and the other somewhere in Africa. The idea is to focus upon the similarities between the two parts of the world. Unfortunately the book is simplistic and compares a stereotype white middle class child with the life of a child in a less economically developed African village. Neither of the images can give the whole picture and certainly Africa as a large continent with huge cultural diversity and richness of civilisation cannot be portrayed in such a manner.

The selection of books to ensure a gender balance and to avoid stereotyping roles and responsibilities is an important task for the teacher. Two books which could contribute to discussions are first, *Giant* by Juliet and Charles Snape, a moral tale about how humans fail to care for the earth. They pollute and despoil the land, and having almost wrecked their environment, are rescued by Mother Earth.

Second, *Dear Daddy* by Phillippe Dupasquier is a story about a father who works on a ship and travels around the world. The book very effectively shows on one half of each page his family carrying on their lives and work at home in the U.K. whilst the other half shows him going about his life and work aboard ship. But what messages do these books convey?

Using Children's Literature in the Classroom

Some examples of contexts in which literature was used

A whole Primary School issue based study of the environment
  Dinosaurs and all that Rubbish, by Michael Foreman.
This moral tale about the way people treat the planet was used in a Primary School as the starting point for a whole school investigation into the school's environment and the immediate locality and how they were being altered by a number of factors. These included the dropping of litter, the usage of a newly constructed playground and the impact of a new road and hypermarket development on a greenfield site adjacent to the school.

A class topic at Key Stage 1 covering a locality beyond the U.K.
  The Village of Square and Round Houses, by Ann Grifalconi,
  supported by *Volcano, Eyewitness Guides No. 38.*
The story line for this book is described later in the chapter, but the key elements of its use include the following:

First, it does provide an interesting and sometimes exciting story about life in another part of the world, in a locality which is in marked contrast with the lives of most children in the U.K. In particular it draws attention to the benefits and costs of living near an active volcano. The story allows children to know and understand what it is like to live in such an environment. The story also provides many opportunities for art and drama as well as for creative writing in engaging the learner.

Second, the story gives another image of Africa – a huge continent with many contrasting environments and cultures. On its own it could be said to give a rather an unbalanced view of life on the continent, but bearing in mind the impression the pictures of starvation and destruction which often fill our TV screens make upon our images of Africa it is right to give a range of alternative ideas. The evidence from the use of this book is that the children are fascinated by the pace of life and how it compares with their own rather hurried existence.

Third, the children are just beginning their detailed investigation of other places and this book offers a large number of points of comparison with their own lives, many of which are concerned with similarities rather than differences.

As the basis for a class topic at Key Stage 1 for skill development
Each Peach, Pear, Plum, by Janet and Allan Ahlberg.
This book is about the imaginary world of story-book characters. At the beginning there is a large double page spread which shows a landscape in which all the stories take place. Each of the stories further explores this landscape in both text and picture. However, each of these explorations of the original picture are drawn from a different angle. The author has seen the book used in a very imaginative way, where the children have applied a range of geographical skills involving the interpretation of pictures and the construction of maps linked to the description of landscapes. Each of the separate images and stories was related back to the original picture. This also involved the use of an enlargement of the double page spread in the form of a wall display which was labelled with a set of symbols devised by the children.

As a book box collection from the library service on the theme of threatened environments and in particular the rain forest – a course for Year 5/6 children
The course was centred around two key books: *Rainforest*, by Helen Cowcher, and *Trees Rule OK*, by Sue Limb.
The children used the latter to provide an example of an issue at the local scale in the U.K. to compare with the issues raised by the massive changes to the rainforest ecology. A good linkage between the local and global scales and offering a real challenge to the values and attitudes of older junior age children.

A topic on a range of Australian environments led by a visiting teacher
This was supported by a wide range of Australian literature which was intended to provide the children with an insight into other cultures and situations both similar and different to life in the U.K. The teacher used the images developed by such TV 'soaps' as *Home and Away* and *Neighbours* as a starting point and then proceeded to use the writing of white and aboriginal authors to explore and develop a set of alternative ideas and views of Australia today.

In addition, Anne Gadsden (1991), has produced a useful analysis of five stories for Key Stage 1 children which include key questions and suggested activities for the children.

Strategies for Using Literature in the Classroom

The use of literature in the classroom needs to be put in the broader educational context of storytelling and story writing. Stories are widely used in the primary classroom and the reasons for doing so are discussed in detail by Horner and Lincoln (1993). Two reasons are quoted here, as they emphasise the role in which literature may be used in the primary geography classroom. They emphasise social cohesion in the classroom, at a local level and nationally and internationally.

'In a multi-ethnic society such as ours, the sharing of stories from many different cultures not only enriches our experience, but makes a contribution to a harmonious multi-cultural society.'

'Storytelling is a powerful socially cohesive activity contributing to the overall climate for oracy within the classroom and via links with adults outside the school, a bridge to the wider community.'

Horner and Lincoln make the following points with regard to stories and geography – they can emphasise the power of place, the cultural background to the story, and the common themes which run through all the stories regardless of culture. They list love, hate, family, fear and betrayal; to which one could add the more geographical characteristics – shelter, fuel, water, food and security. These could all be talking points when reading a story to children and could be points for the individual reader to note.

There are a number of ways in which stories can be managed to involve the learner and these include:

(i) Discussion about the story: Where was it located? What is the place or environment like? What happened to whom? What changes occurred and how were they caused? What things were the same and what things were different as compared with life where you live? What is your opinion about what happened in the story?

(ii) The use of stories told by adults: these are particularly important when looking at change over time in the local area. These stories can be integrated to give a wider perspective on the locality, its form, characteristics and change over time.

(iii) Stories, particularly about environmental issues, can be told without the ending; the children then have to consider a possible range of outcomes and compare them with that of the author.

(iv) The production of maps, models, or both, to record and locate places, events and journeys in the story.

(v) The locations of where a range of stories are from could be recorded on a map not only to locate the place, but to develop a wide geographic spread from around the U.K. and further afield.

(vi) The children could devise a form of passport which could be 'stamped' as they visit a new place, country or environment in a story.

(vii) A geographical vocabularly with definitions, could be built-up in the form of a wall display.

(viii) Writing a story as a class, group or individual child about an environment and locality known to them with the intention of sharing it with other children in schools either in the U.K. or further afield.

Progression and the Use of Literature

The choice of literature is the teacher's and is related to the intended use. The key issue is to ensure that the use enables the children to build upon their prior learning.

One of the key elements in planning the geography curriculum is to determine how investigations, knowledge and understanding developed in Key Stage 1 can be built on and extended in Key Stage 2. This is discussed in *An Introduction to Teaching Geography at Key Stages 1 and 2* (NCC 1993, Chapter 5). Eight ways of achieving progression in geography are suggested and these include: the move from the concrete and specific to more generalised and abstract matters; and a developing awareness of social, political and environmental issues.

This progression may be demonstrated in a study of the home locality at Key Stages 1 and 2. The work at Key Stage 1 could involve the use of *Anno's Counting Book* by Mitsumasa Anno, and at Key Stage 2 *The Revenge of Samuel Stokes* by Penelope Lively. The former is a picture book composed of twelve double page spreads which show the progressive development of a settlement from a bare landscape with a river flowing through it to a small town with churches, roads and railways. This could be used to help infant age children to understand, possibly with the addition of a hardware model, how settlements including their own locality might have grown over time. The latter book is an account of how a new housing estate is built on the site of a park designed by a fictional landscape architect, Samuel Stokes. He and his park keep reappearing as ghosts in the landscape. It is a humorous story, but as Tim, one of the main characters in the story, considers:

'For hundreds of years. Or not, as the case might be. Tim thought again of successions of places, all on the same bit of ground: forests, maybe, and then fields, and then houses, and then something grand and a bit mad like Samuel Stokes' park and then more houses and gardens...'

This could be used in Key Stage 2 to explore how changes in our locality are not always welcomed by everyone and that development issues can be complex and sometimes controversial.

Assessment and the Use of Literature

Over the past three years, many primary school teachers have extended their capabilities with the use of children's literature by using it for assessment, particularly at Key Stage 1.

The following is included as an example of how geography might be assessed through the use of a book which is probably familiar to most classroom practitioners, *Lucy And Tom at the Seaside*, by Shirley Hughes. For many children, the visit to a beach is probably one of the most memorable experiences of early childhood. It is generally a large space in which they can create and destroy sandcastles and the like and can run in and out of the water, something which is generally not possible at the swimming baths. The geography of the meeting ground between the open sea and land is very dynamic and subject to observable changes. (See also the example in *Pupils Work Assessed in Geography and History at Key Stages 1 and 2* (SEAC 1993)). Not only that, but the broad principles may be demonstrated relatively easily in the wet area of the classroom. Some quotes from the story are linked to aspects of the physical geography:

'The sea is much roughier and splashier than the swimming pool near home' – *wave action and erosion.*

'The tide is coming in. Dad helps Lucy and Tom to make a beautiful sandcastle...Slowly the moat fills up with water, then the tunnel. Soon only the turret is left. Then nothing at all.' – *tidal movement and wave erosion, deposition and transport.*

'Lucy and Tom play in a rock pool' – *the product of erosion filled with water left behind by the falling tide.*

Surely at Key Stage 1 such books can be used to explore through the use of discussion, brief written accounts, drawing and drama, the understanding which children have gained about the physical environment and how it affects their lives.

The Use of Children's and Other Literature for INSET

There are a number of very strong reasons for using children's literature as a basis for some geography related in-service training (INSET). The main aim for most INSET related to the primary curriculum is to demonstrate to teachers, many of whom stopped studying geography at the age of 14 or even younger, how they might plan, develop and resource the National Curriculum.

Using literature for aiding the professional development process uses other attributes of teachers which are related to a broad curriculum planning expertise, coupled with a mature and informed outlook on the world.

Adults are often confident readers of literature and will already use that expertise within school life: in the classroom, in assemblies and amongst colleagues. The use of literature at storytime is one of the main ways in which the teacher comes into a close working relationship with the whole class, allowing all concerned to share ideas and reactions in a relaxed and friendly atmosphere. In particular, in recent years teachers of Year 2 children have developed wide ranging expertise in the use of literature, partly through the Key Stage 1 National Curriculum assessment. Using literature for Geography INSET is a natural development of that expertise, placing the teacher in control of information and ideas generated by the discussions about the books chosen. These discussions encourage them to develop ideas, many of which have a geographical connotation and which often derive from an awareness and use of the local area, coupled with personal travel, and professional training and experience.

Children's literature is a relatively easily available resource and most primary classrooms or libraries possess a range of suitable titles. It could therefore be a case of using what is already available in the school before embarking on the purchasing of curriculum materials.

The strongest case for using literature is that it is one way of putting geography within a whole school and whole curriculum context, something which reassures colleagues faced with new curriculum content and limited curriculum time and resources, but who would wish to provide their children with a coherent curriculum experience. It helps to make curriculum links which are not detrimental to the understanding of geography by the teacher and the taught. On the contrary, these links help to demonstrate a strong case for geography within the primary school because it provides a context for learning across the curriculum, from the world of the school and its grounds, the local area and to other places both near and far.

A practical example of using literature for INSET

The example derives from the experience gained in School- and Centre-based INSET. It has tended to be most successful with groups of twelve or less as this still allows for all concerned to contribute freely.

The content of the diagrammatic presentation on pages 152 and 153 has been used by the author to structure discussions of a geographical and curriculum nature.

152

DISCUSSIONS OF A CURRICULUM NATURE

How children's literature might be used to help in construction of the curriculum, and to aid geographical understanding by teachers.

ii. Consider how the use of a range of literature might be used to extend and complement the coverage of places and environments within the curriculum. In particular, to provide an increased opportunity for comparisons in terms of similarity and difference between your locality and the local environment and other localities and environments. Consider also the corrolary – what resources might be necessary to extend the effective use of literature in the primary geography curriculum?

i. Action research: How might the literature be used for story time and/or as a set of books available as class readers. Jointly agree a literature collection to explore its effectiveness with children of different ages and abilities. Compare outcomes at a future meeting.

i. What are the characteristic features of the place or the environment:
– is it in the countryside or a town?
– are there any human features such as roads, shops?
– are there any physical features such as slopes, hills, valleys?
– are there any pictures which give clear images of the nature of the place?
– are there maps or plans which give an idea of layout and form of the place?

ii. Is it a made or natural environment? – made means affected to a greater or lesser extent by people.

iii. Are there reasons why the place is situated where it is?
– is it on a hill, or by a stream, or by the sea or somewhere else?
– is it on a main road, or near a town, or village or somewhere else?

iv. Is the place or environment subject to changes either made or natural?
– are there any physical changes such as the weather, climate and the seasons, or earth movements or erosion or deposition by water, ice and wind?
– are there any changes caused by human actions?

DISCUSSIONS OF A GEOGRAPHICAL NATURE
Questions about places and environments in children's literature

iii. Consider how the literature might be used to develop an awareness and understanding of language and culture in a multi-ethnic U.K., and as part of developing an understanding of the wealth of languages, cultures and environments on a world scale.

iv. How might the use of literature be more formally built into the curriculum in terms of such matters as: when is it most appropriate and in what learning context?; how can literature be used to support progression and how may it be used for assessment? Where in the curriculum?

An example of children's literature

v. How might the use of other poetry and literature be used to extend the geographical awareness and understanding of fellow colleagues?

Babylon, by Jill Paton Walsh.
A story about three children of Afro-Caribbean origin, one of whom was born in the U.K., and their adventures in exploring their local environment in inner-city London. This book is full of talking points and curriculum opportunities, but any use in the classroom would need to be sensitively handled by the teacher. The book offers an insight into another locality which for many children in England and Wales could be described, in national curriculum terms, as a 'contrasting locality in the U.K.'

viii Where is this place or environment?

vii. Does the book portray life in other cultures and ethnic groups?
– are these aspects portrayed sensitively without being either patronising or over-simplistic?
– who wrote the book and what is their experience of the place or environment?

v. Is the place large or small, important or unimportant?

vi. In what ways is the place or environment similar to or different from your home locality or other localities you know?

Conclusion

This chapter has shown how children's literature offers a valuable resource not only to provide information about places and environments, but also to enthuse and interest children in their world and to encourage them to look more closely and to write more expressively about their existence on this planet.

Literature can provide teachers with a valuable source of ideas for discussion which helps them to explore the curriculum, in particular the contribution made by geography.

Storybooks about places

A compilation of titles from Cheshire 20-Day Geography Course members, Kate Campion and Jeremy Krause.

Collections of stories from around the world

'Tales from the Caribbean' – The Beginning of things; 'Tales from the Caribbean' – Anansi Stories; 'Tales from the Caribbean' – Witches and Duppies; 'Tales from the Caribbean' – Stories from history. All by Evan Jones. Ginn.

'Stories from Overseas' – from Zambia/Kenya/India/Malaysia/Tanzania and Nepal – four books. Published by Malvern Oxfam Group, 18 Church Street, Malvern, Worcs WR14 2AY.

'Fairy tales from near and far' by Amabel Williams-Ellis. Blackie.

'West Indian Folk tales' – Retold by Philip Sherlock. Oxford University Press.

'African Myths and Legends' – Retold by Kathleen Arnott. Oxford University Press.

'Indian Tales and Legends' – Retold by J. E. B. Gray. Oxford University Press.

'Time for telling' – stories from around the world. Selected by M. Medlicott. Kingfisher Books.

Poems and Songs

'Let's celebrate' – festival poems. Compiled by John Foster. Oxford University Press.

'The Singing Sack' – song stories from around the world. Compiled by Helen East. A and C Black.

Journeys

'A balloon for Grandad' by Nigel Gray. Collins Picture Lions.

'Sammy goes flying' by Odette Elliott. Puffin Books.

'Anno's Journey' by Mitsumasa Anno. The Bodley Head.
'The Fantastic Flying Journey' by Gerald Durrell. Conran Octopus Ltd.

Stories about particular places
'A thief in the village' (Jamaica) by James Berry. Puffin.
'The most beautiful place in the world' (Guatemala) by Ann Cameron. Young Corgi.
'The Haunted Coast' (Dunwich, Suffolk) by Su Swallow. Anglia Young Books.
'Coming Home' (USA-Ireland) by Martin Waddell and Neil Reed. Simon & Schuster.
'Waiting for Anya' (The Pyrenees) by Michael Morpurgo. Heinemann.
'Underground to Canada' by Barbara Smucker. Puffin.
'Flames in the forest' (India) by Ruskin Bond. Puffin.
'Under the Hawthorn Tree' (famine in Ireland) by Marita Conlon-McKenna. Viking.
'The Middle of Somewhere' (A story of South Africa) by Sheila Gordon. Orchard.
'Charlie's House' (South African township) by Reviva Schermbrucker. Walker Books.
'The Cow that fell into the canal' (The Netherlands) by Phyllis Krasilovsky. Puffin.

Imaginary Places or Fact or Fiction?
'Little Water and the Gift of the Animals' by C. J. Taylor. Tundra Books.
'The Bunyip of Berkeley's Creek' by Jenny Wagner. Picture Puffin.
'Whale is stuck' by Charles Fuge and Karen Hayles. BBC Books.
'Stories for five year olds' – Edited by Sara and Stephen Corrin. Puffin.

Conservation of the environment
'The World that Jack built' by Ruth Brown. Red Fox.
'Bringing the rain to the Kapiti Plain' by Verna Aardema. Macmillan.

Non fiction
Oliver and Boyd Geography
   'Living on Islands', 'Cold Places', 'Hot Places'.
'Exploring Caribbean Food in Britain' by Floella Benjamin. Mantra Publishing.
'African Food and Drink' by M. Gibrill. Wayland.
'Indian Food and Drink' by V. P. Kanitkar. Wayland.
'Caribbean Food and Drink' by Aviva Paraiso. Wayland.

CHAPTER 12

Primary Geography and the European Dimension

Jo Hughes and Keith Paterson

Introduction

The founding father of the European Community, Jean Monet, recognised the benefits of a European dimension in education. He declared on one occasion that if he had to start again to launch the Community he would begin with education. Today the benefits of European awareness are readily acknowledged, whether related to primary, secondary or tertiary levels of education. For the majority of primary teachers this is, however, a new area, a problematic field, difficult to cultivate. This chapter explores the issues involved with implementing a European dimension in primary school geography. It traces the recent development of European awareness in the curriculum, and then focuses on how European awareness can be developed and resourced in a geographical context.

The Context

Interest in the European dimension in education was triggered when Britain entered the European Economic Community in 1973. During the last five years or so this interest has revived in a period of dramatic change, occasioned by new developments within Europe and change in the national context. The significant developments which have shaped the current state of play can be traced to two major influences: closer political and economic ties with Europe; and European Community resolutions. Of course a third major influence, so far as schools are concerned, is the impact of the National Curriculum.

Ties with Europe

Since the Treaty of Rome, ratified in 1957, the European Community has grown in scope, size and ambition. For the United Kingdom, accession in 1973 meant greater involvement in European affairs, more contacts, more trade and less insularity. The Single European Act of 1986, approved by the British Parliament in 1989, established the framework for the completion of the internal market, a market without barriers, allowing free movement of people, goods, capital and services. For the 344 million inhabitants in the twelve nations of the European Community, the Single European Act represents the most tangible evidence of 'Brusselization', from which the manifestly stronger impact of Brussels on the British way of life has largely emerged.

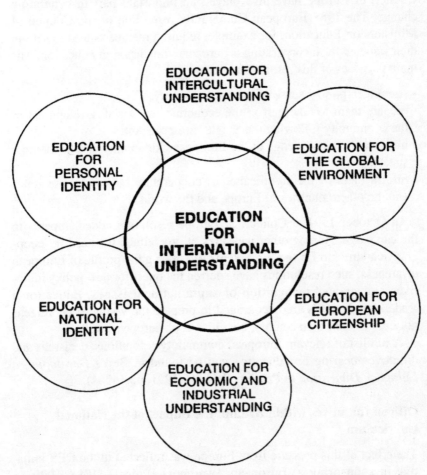

Figure 12.1: Elements of the European dimension (After Bell and Dransfield, 1992)

The Treaty of Maastricht of 1991 paved the way for even closer economic and political unity, and is now approved by all member states. It includes sections *(Articles 126 and 127)* on education. These Articles complement the member states' efforts to provide 'quality education', through cooperation on a broad spectrum of issues and the development of a European dimension (Figure 12.1). They open up new possibilities for closer cooperation at all levels of education, in recognition that education can spearhead cooperation and partnership in other areas of activity.

European Community and Council of Europe Resolutions

Specific resolutions emanating from the European Community and the Council of Europe have also played an important part in generating change. The 1988 European Community resolution of the Council of Ministers on Education, for example, required member states to set out their policies for incorporating a European dimension in education. The main purposes of this resolution were to:

- strengthen pupils' sense of European identity;
- prepare them to take part in the economic and social development of the community following the Single European Act;
- improve their knowledge of the European Community and its member states;
- inform them of the significance of cooperation between those states and the other countries of Europe and the world.

In October 1991, a Council of Europe resolution added impetus to the campaign. Among other measures, it proclaimed the need for cooperative address to Europe's problems. By raising the profile of European awareness, such resolutions have spurred the quest for new policy initiatives and greater recognition of supra-national issues. Educational leaders at all levels are encouraged to prepare the young to be citizens not only of their own country, but citizens of Europe as well.

A full list of relevant European community resolutions, decisions and directives bearing on education can be found in Bell's *Developing a European Dimension in Primary Schools* (1991, pp.142–4).

Official Initiatives within Britain: the Impact of the National Curriculum

The effect of this pressure from Europe was reflected in the DES initiative in sponsoring a 'European Awareness Project' (1988–1990), a curriculum development intiative in twelve local authorities in the

United Kingdom. It considered policy models for the provision of European awareness, and suggested ways of making more effective use of resources, and the promotion of good practice within a range of educational establishments.

The National Curriculum discussions from the late 1980s have also reflected the need to take account of the promotion of the European dimension. During this period the National Curriculum Council established a task group to examine the implications of the European dimension for citizenship as a cross-curricular theme. The European dimension in fact was evident in a number of the Council's cross-curricular guidance documents. Thus in *Curriculum Guidance 3: the Whole Curriculum* (1990), it declared that teachers 'have a major role in preparing young people for adult life: this means life in a multicultural, multi-lingual Europe which, in its turn, is interdependent with the rest of the world.' (p.3).

Similarly, in *Curriculum Guidance 4: Economic and Industrial Understanding* (1990), a means was offered of exploring the context of the Single European Act. Geography was seen as having a significant role to play in introducing children in a tangible way to the living and working environments of our European partners. In doing so it would help to fulfil a major objective of education for economic and industrial understanding, by exploring the concepts at local, national, European and global perspectives. Likewise, many of the themes in *Curriculum Guidance 7: Environmental Education* (1990), provided an ideal vehicle for permeating European issues into geography, such as the impact of human activities on the environment in the European context. Linking with both these guidance documents were recommendations in *Curriculum Guidance 8: Education for Citizenship* (1990), which again suggested a concentric scheme for promoting a knowledge and understanding of different communities, from family and school at the local level, to national, European and global scales. Primary geography can therefore move hand in hand with the international dimension of citizenship, in which European awareness plays an important role, with, on the face of it, official blessing.

The Education Reform Act of 1988 led to the establishment of working groups for each subject which it had identified as contributing to a statutory National Curriculum, and the Council of Ministers resolution of 1988 was part of the terms of reference of the working groups. In its Interim Report (November 1989), the Geography Working Group devoted one Attainment Target (AT3 'The United Kingdom within the European Community') to the European dimension. The Attainment Targets were reduced in the Final Report, which offered a broader approach to place studies, AT2 Knowledge and Understanding of Places, in which, for the primary phase, at Key Stage 2, there was specific reference to a locality study in the European Community. Unfortunately, at a very late stage in the procedure, the Secretary of State for Education limited this locality study to Level 5, potentially marginalising it for many primary schools.

In February 1991 the government published its policy of activities undertaken to implement the Council of Ministers 1988 resolution. Among its objectives it included the need for pupils 'to acquire a view of Europe as a multicultural, multi-lingual community which includes the United Kingdom'. In March 1992 the Department for Education updated its guidance on policy models and detailed key concerns pertaining to the implementation of European dimension policies in LEAs, schools and colleges. Four broad objectives for a school policy were suggested:

• knowledge and understanding of Europe, its peoples and its place in the world;
• positive but critical attitudes towards other peoples and cultures;
• respect for different ways of life, beliefs, opinions and ideas;
• enhanced language capability to facilitate communication and cooperation. (p.8)

In the same year, the DfE produced a schools pack entitled *The European Dimension*, which testified to official acceptance in a more practical approach to some possibilities available to schools of exploring the European dimension in the context of the National Curriculum.

Clearly the lack of a modern language element in the official primary curriculum limits the achievement of the fourth objective in this phase. It draws attention, however, to the value of teachers having a second language, even at a basic level, in the context of school exchanges and organised excursions to Europe. It is also vital in any European studies unit to include resource material in the relevant original language, even for young children.

Implementing the European Dimension in Primary Schools

Starting them Young: Attacking Stereotypes

Until recently, European studies have mainly been a secondary and higher education activity. Primary schools have generally been less involved. As part of a contribution to broader international understanding, however, it is vital that primary school children participate in curriculum developments which address the European dimension. It has been recognised for some time that attitudes and values have already been formed, even rigidly so, by the time children reach secondary school. Children are more likely to be open to new ideas and experiences at primary level. This broader dimension is also intrinsic to a progressive personal and social education policy, encouraging young children to become decreasingly egocentric and more aware of their relationship with others, following a concentric process (see Chapter 7) of moving out from their homes and schools to their broader locality and community, then to the national and international level.

It would seem particularly important that children of an island nation, prone to developing insular attitudes, should be encouraged to regard themselves as part of Europe, apart from the political and economic influences. A piece of research undertaken between 1982 and 1987 (Ovens, in Bell et al., 1989) showed that our pupils were disadvantaged by their lack of direct contact with mainland Europe. Attitudes and beliefs about Europe were found to be often over-simple and distorted, but were nevertheless firmly formed and expressed. They were unlikely to develop an empathy towards Europe on the basis of written materials alone, however. A vital interest in Europe was closely related to the quality and amount of actual contact with things and people European.

More of today's children of primary age are in contact with Europe than ever before, either through television programmes or through holidays in Europe. At the same time, these experiences characteristically offer negative slants. The images and impressions of a place visited can leave a negative stereotype, especially if the visit was restricted to a popular tourist area, geared to providing a generalised global culture of hamburgers and fries and 'English pubs' on the one hand, and hot sunny beaches and local exotica for tourists on the other. One advantage of the Blanes case study (Chapter 5) is that the resort is less commercialised and more used for holidays by local people than by the international market, and therefore is less untypical of Spain than the high profile resorts such as Benidorm.

A useful way of approaching a study of more distant peoples is to provide a contrast with the child's own experiences. As a pedagogical tool, the power of contrast was emphasised by Bruner, as a means of encouraging children to look with a fresh eye at their own familiar situations.

'by getting a child to explore contrasts he is more likely to organise his knowledge in a fashion that helps discovery...its efficacy stems from the fact that a concept requires for its definition a choice of a negative case' (Bruner, 1963, p.15)

While Bruner is in essence correct, his choice of terminology we now see as anachronistic. A better way of putting it is that children begin to acquire concepts through distinguishing examples from non-examples (as in the case of a mountain and a hill in Chapter 7). One problem of contrasts is that, as they have often done in the past, they produce positive stereotypes of the familiar area and negative ones of the distant place. In this context, a more appropriate way is to explore similarities and differences. Thus in the Blanes case study even young children could be asked to find similarities first, then differences, between their home resort, say Bridlington, and the foreign one, Blanes.

A European dimension can be addressed through themes at different levels of complexity, particularly through subject areas such as geography and history and, of course, in language. In geography, examples are weather and climate, transport and communications, food, homes, occupations and leisure activities. Environmental issues can also effectively be covered. Indeed, the problem of the European locality study being left to Level 5 can be circumvented by choosing a European locality as an overseas study at Key Stage 1, and also by the regular use of European examples in the coverage of geographical skills and themes, also illustrated in the Blanes study.

Cross-phase Links

As already noted, language is a major facilitator of links with countries that, though close to us economically, politically and culturally, have different languages. While a modern language is not formally required in the primary school, a good European awareness project must surely involve some relevant second language work, even if only at the kind of 'survival', phrase book level, as acquired by many tourists. In this context, it is useful for primary and secondary schools to establish cross-phase links for European awareness, with a modern language specialist from the secondary school helping with the cluster of its feeder primary schools.

This happened with a secondary school and some feeder primary schools in Southport, joining forces to produce their own newspaper, as part of an already thriving 'Newspaper in Education' cross-phase project. Funding was available from the Central Bureau on European Exchanges through the LEA. The secondary school hosted two days of European awareness to which the primary schools were invited. Children were involved in food tasting, currency dealing, other role play, games, dancing, singing, drama and puppet theatre, the various activities based on the culture of different European countries. The secondary school purchased resources for the project which can in future be loaned to the feeder primary schools.

Many pupils wrote articles for their newspaper about these two days, about school visits to Europe and their own holidays there as well. The potential of cross-curricular links, as well as the valuable cross-phase link, between geography, language and economic awareness, was explored in the context of Europe. Children of different age groups learned much about cooperative work in the planning, drafting and production of a newspaper, and therefore a contribution to industrial understanding. A high level of motivation was engendered. As two eleven year olds wrote:

> The play was brilliant: it challenged all the stereotypes about Europe and it was really funny...the whole thing made you think about what we imagine other European people to be like and what they think of us.'

European Links and Exchanges: the Twinning Principle

There can be little doubt that one of the most productive ways of fostering a European dimension in the primary school is through a link or exchange with a partner, or twinned, school abroad. The word exchange is used in the very broadest sense of the exchange of materials and ideas, and the movement of individuals and groups. In fully fledged twinning arrangements, both will be involved. But there is great potential benefit also in a more limited contact through correspondence.

For those considering an exchange for the first time there are a number of sources of guidance. Thus Savage (1992) offers a practical, step-by-step approach. This is complemented by the Central Bureau's publication, *Making the Most of your Partner School*. One obvious tactic is to make use of any twinning arrangement your local place has with a European location. Established town twinning schemes may offer community-wide support on both sides. Some LEAs have created support systems for twinning, both at the European scale and beyond, as, for example, Avon (Beddis and Mares, 1988). Cheshire LEA has mapped the impressive range of twinning contacts between its schools and contrasted localities within the county and the country at large, and with Europe. For many teachers, however, the trigger will simply be personal contact, a friend or relative in Europe, a fellow teacher or governor, or one established while on a field visit or a holiday.

Once this initial contact has been made, expansion can profitably be at a number of levels, ranging from the class, to the school, to the wider community, the multiplier effect bringing with it a shared sense of purpose. Good communications are as essential as a joint commitment to the success of a twinning arrangement. Correspondence using normal postal services is obviously the most frequent method, to exchange messages, diaries, personal information, data about the home town and region, weather, maps, photographs, school projects and surveys, newspaper cuttings, comics, artwork, stories and songs, audio and video cassette recordings, as well as the printed word and still photographs. A great advantage is that return material will include, on the one hand, features expressing similarity, and other material drawing attention to differences, particularly language.

Increasingly, more immediate and technological advanced forms of communication are being introduced. One, no doubt on a limited scale owing to its cost, is contact by telephone. Another is the availability of facsimile transmission facilities, offering new opportunities for rapid and relatively low cost communication. Electronic mail, which uses a computer to generate a message to send to a distant 'mail box' is of potential significance for the future, though few primary schools have such a facility at present.

Such links are of prime importance in creating a living European dimension within the school. They will no doubt be geared towards the specific demands of the National Curriculum such as, in geography, establishing the link to generate the required European locality study, for which it offers a richer range of resources than might otherwise have been acquired.

Coordinating the European Dimension: INSET Support

For any complicated piece of whole curriculum planning, as the European dimension implies, it is important for there to be a member of staff who can take overall responsibility for the planning, implementation, monitoring and evaluation of the process. A particularly important function of the coordinator is to audit existing good practice, as suggested in the NCC guidance document on *The Whole Curriculum* (p.17). The coordination role can only successfully be assumed where the support of the headteacher and colleages is present, and where some funding is made available (not least of time) to resource the initiative. In the small primary school there will clearly not be the resource for a separate coordinator for each area, and the person responsible for the European dimension will need to be attached also to other subjects, which could appropriately be geography or history, or both.

Bearing in mind the pressures of a widely acknowledged surfeit of content in the National Curriculum, it may be thought that introducing the European dimension is a peripheral luxury. Successful coordination will, however, make clear the benefits of permeating an integrated European dimension, through subsidiary topics, into a wide range of subject areas and cross-curricular themes and dimensions. Without such coordination, the almost limitless opportunities that the European dimension generates may result in unfocused and/or idiosyncratic use by individual teachers, failure to build-in continuity and progression, and possible duplication or, more likely in an overcrowded timetable, neglect. The ideal is to plan for progression in European awareness on the basis of something like the *spiral curriculum* suggested in Chapter 7, ensuring there are clearly defined links between it and other parts of the curriculum, matched to the different levels at Key Stages 1 and 2.

To obviate the likelihood of ill-planned European dimension work, the coordinator needs to have access to INSET time, both for her- or himself attending INSET courses and conferences, and for the follow-up school-based INSET. It may be useful to invite persons with whom contact has been made in external INSET activity, whether an LEA adviser, a secondary teacher or a member of staff from an institution of higher education, who have expertise in the European dimension, to come to the school. This can make a contribution to a forward-looking curriculum development plan and the ongoing internal INSET provided as part of staff professional development.

One element of curriculum change that is important to monitor is not just the presence of a curriculum initiative such as European awareness in the curriculum, but also whether there have been changes of percep-tions and attitudes as a result of it. The most fruitful way of achieving this is arranging for visits to Europe. But is this practical as part of INSET? A positive example of this might be cited: part of a recent GEST 20–day course in primary geography, which the GIPP team coor-dinate, working with advisers from five LEAs in the North-west. GEST funding from the DfE provided for supply time for the staff attending the course at the rate of approximately £100 a day. It was found that if the teachers were prepared to travel in holiday time, in this case in the autumn half-term, a four day visit could be arranged at a slightly cheaper rate than four days of supply during term-time. The visit was based on Barcelona, and included studies of the geography of particular localities in Catalonia and, not least, of Catalonian culture and ways of life as part of the broader European dimension. The materials collected were not only designed to meet the needs of the schools of particular teachers, whether at Key Stage 1 or Key Stage 2, but were also included in a formal assignment, part of the work required for a University of Liverpool Certificate in Primary Geography. Thus the work was not only of critical value to the school, both for geography, other National

Curriculum subjects (such as art) and for cross-curricular themes and dimensions, but was accredited as a part of the teacher's own personal development profile. Not least, there was a manifest recognition of the value and interest of the authentic geographical input offered, by non-specialist primary teachers.

An important part of the preparation of the organising team was therefore to demonstrate that these geographical insights into the region and its localities were a critical 'resource'. The more obvious resources: maps, photographs and the like, were means to this end. The resources were addressed to the level of the teacher. A priority for the teacher was to filter the material and reconstitute it in the form of schemes of work and activities suitable for children of different age groups, and also to gear it to the relevant requirements of the National Curriculum. The Blanes case study in Chapter 5 is one example of the type of preliminary work that was necessary.

Suggestions for Resource-based Activities

Broadening the discussion out from the Catalonia example to the larger European dimension, Bell and Dransfield (1992) have identified the following principles in developing a European awareness programme:

- commence with what is familiar to the children;
- involve the children in planning the project, posing their own questions and directing their own work;
- develop resource-based learning skills, required to extract information from maps, photographs, diagrams and other sources;
- provide scope both for individual and group work;
- use classroom visitors with particular knowledge and understanding of Europe to generate enthusiasm.

Examples of Resource-based Activities

1 Collecting **photographs** of people and places from particular countries. Ask children to describe what they see on the photographs. Get them to ask each other questions on these photographs. Discuss similarities and differences in photographs placed in the correct locations round a large plastic **map of Europe**. Prepare stickers of names of particular countries to label them on the map. Ask the children what they know about these countries and whether they have visited them. Ask how they would get to them from their own area.

2 Choose **one country** and explore a particular theme, such as **food** and **recipes.** Taste bread derived from different countries, e.g. baguettes,

croissants, garlic bread and rye bread. Work out a menu of European foods that could be cooked in school. What foods can be found on the supermarket shelves coming from particular countries? How could we tell in a supermarket which country we were in? Collect labels of food produced in other countries in Europe, and prepare them for a display. Each country has a bar code written on all its goods. That for Britain is '5', the 5 coming before the other numbers. Discover the numbers for other countries, and say which item of food you found them on.

3 The **European Community:** mark the names of the EC countries on a large map of Europe together with their capital cities. Mark on also the biggest rivers and mountain ranges. When and why was the European Community established? Find out some of the advantages and disadvantages of being in the European Community.

4 The **Channel Tunnel:** Why was the Channel tunnel built? Why was it very costly to build? Which countries will it connect? What sorts of traffic will go through it? What effect will it have on: (a) the ferry crossing of the English Channel; and (b) air connections between Britain and Europe? How will it affect the environment of England and France? In what ways may the link help us to become more European?

5 Physical Geography – the **weather and flora and fauna of Europe:** compare the weather and climate of the local area with that of the part of Europe being studied. What are the similarities and differences between the crops, natural vegetation and animal life of Britain and those of the Mediterranean part of Europe? How are these related to the climate? Find out if there are species threatened with extinction, and why. What measures are being taken to conserve these species?

6 **Language, stories and music:** find out in your class whether any of the children and their families speak a European language. How and why have they learnt it? Debate the advantages of knowledge of a foreign language. Why do more foreigners seem to speak English than English people can speak a foreign language? In which other parts of the world is a European language spoken? Why? Find out about minority languages within different countries. Why do these exist? Find stories and folk tales from different European countries. Respond to these in drawing and writing. Why does a lot of the music we enjoy come from Europe? What sorts of music come from particular countries (e.g. Spain)? Why do we get Christmas carols from many different European countries?

7 **International links:** What raw materials and resources which Europe needs are brought from other parts of the world? Why do not European countries produce these resources themselves? Find out and label on a large map the routes followed by ships bringing these materials into European countries. Why does Europe seem to gain more from these links than such economically developing countries? Why are there large numbers of immigrants from other parts of the world in European countries? Name some of these immigrants and the routes they need to follow to get from their home country.

Conclusion

Despite the overcrowded nature of the primary curriculum, recently reduced in the implementation of the Dearing Report, promotion of a European dimension is an important element in whole curriculum planning. It is needed in the current context to provide the entitlement of a broad, balanced and relevant curriculum for all primary children. A structured framework of curriculum links can be worked out for each contributing topic. The main problem is that there are too many to choose from.

The main criteria we have noted for working out and implementing a policy that deals adequately at least with the European dimension are:

- careful planning by a coordinator well-versed in the issues related to European awareness;
- links with a partner school in Europe;
- actual visits to the locality of this school and surrounding areas;
- a spiral curriculum scheme which allows revisiting the European themes at progressively more refined levels through the primary school;
- cross-phase links with a secondary school, as appropriate;
- building-in a viable second language element, bearing in mind direct modern language teaching is not formally expected in the primary school;
- up-to-date and accurate knowledge of the workings of the European Community.

The potential of carefully conceived and focused work on Europe is enormous. Geographers can justifiably claim that their subject more than most, if properly used, can help to break down barriers and create a better understanding of more distant places and cultures. Internationalisation of the curriculum has had a long history in geographical study, and it now remains for geography practioners to ensure that it offers full support to the process of establishing a strong European dimension in the primary curriculum, as much at Key Stage 1 as at Key Stage 2.

Useful Addresses

British Council, 10 Spring Gardens, London SW1A 2BN.

Central Bureau for Education Visits and Exchanges, Seymour Mews House, Seymour Mews, London W1H 9PE.

UK Centre for European Education, Seymour Mews House, Seymour Mews, London W1H 9PE.

DfE, Publications Centre, PO Box 2193, London E15 2EU.

The European Movement, Europe House, 158 Buckingham Palace Road, London SW1 9TR.

European Commission House, Jean Monet House, 8 Storeys Gate, London SW1 3AT.

European Parliament Information Office, 2 Queen Anne's Gate, London SW1A 9AA

Geographical Association, International Committee, 343 Fulwood Road, Sheffield S10 3BP.

The London Map Centre, 22 Caxton House, London SW1H 0QU.

Edward Stanford, 12-14 Longacre, London WC2E 9LP.

Town Twinning Association, Local Government International Bureau, 35 Great South Street, London SW1P 3BT.

CHAPTER 13

Geography for Special Children

Jo Hughes and David Thomas

The aim of this chapter is to attempt to reassure teachers that the Geography National Curriculum has a great deal to offer children who in some way need special provision to make it accessible. A recent report by the National Curriculum Council (March 1993) identified four main groups of pupils who provide a challenge for their teachers to give them this entitlement. These groups were not listed in order to categorise or to deny that all pupils have individual needs within the groups, rather to guide and support teachers. All except group 4 (exceptionally able children) have provided a focus for this chapter. The groups consisted of:

1 Pupils with exceptionally severe learning difficulties including those with:

- profound and multiple learning difficulties, some of whom may have associated challenging behaviours;
- exceptionally severe learning difficulties resulting from, for example, multisensory impairment – these pupils may not be considered as having profound and multiple learning difficulties.

2 Pupils with other learning difficulties including those with:

- mild learning difficulties;
- moderate learning difficulties;
- specific learning difficulties;
- emotional and behavioural difficulties.

3 Pupils with physical or sensory impairment.

4 Exceptionally able pupils. (NCC, 1993)

The National Curriculum Council included special children when it spoke of an entitlement curriculum in the Education Reform Act 1988.

It stressed that children with learning difficulties must have full access to the National Curriculum and it is not to be automatically disapplied for children with statements or in special schools.

At first this caused great concern for some. The dilemma was how to provide the entitlement of breadth and balance indicated by the 1988 Act which involves the whole curriculum, not just subjects, for pupils who may need to spend a great deal of time on developmental skills or life skills (Personal and Social Education). It was thought that the curricula of some children may need to be narrow initially whilst time is spent on overcoming a particular developmental problem, i.e. a speech or communication difficulty. Resolving this problem would however help pupils to benefit from a broader curriculum eventually. Life skills or PSE provided another area of concern for adults working with special children as it was not made a core area on their behalf, bearing in mind that so much of their time is spent developing this aspect. As an area, PSE reflects the aims of the National Curriculum as a whole, to:

(a) promote the spiritual, moral, cultural, mental and physical development of pupils at the school and of society;
(b) prepare such pupils for the opportunities, responsibilities and experiences of adult life. (Curriculum Matters 14, 1989)

However by varying the means of approach and planning, PSE – as with other cross-curricular dimensions – can be taught either by permeating various curricular areas or as blocks of activity. Geography links well with both of these approaches, as demonstrated in some examples given later.

Although some form of integration was an initial reaction of some, other teachers were already providing their pupils with geographical experience. In some schools staff have seen the possibility of using parts of the geography curriculum even if in a modified way to provide stimulus for special children to develop conceptually, aid work in sensory development, link with personal and social education, as well as being an enjoyable and worthwhile area in its own right, where appropriate. One of the findings in a National Curriculum Council review showed that 'teachers (of special children) strongly support the entitlement of all pupils to have a broad, balanced and relevant curriculum...' (NCC, 1993).

One of the positive aspects of the National Curriculum has been in focusing more closely on differentiation for all children. Differentiation has and will continue to be vital for special children whether it is through differentiated task, outcome, through teacher intervention, delivery or resources. Smaller steps and different pathways or routes may be necessary for special children but differentiation of teaching method does not imply differentiation of curricular aim.

The Geography National Curriculum has not provided examples of the small steps of development in the understanding of skills and concepts required by some children with special needs, both to aid progression and to emphasise what they can do rather than what they cannot do (although these may emerge from teachers' experiences of teaching National Curriculum geography). The National Curriculum Council did, however, provide some guidance on differentiation. The need for extra guidance 'on differentiating teaching and learning for all pupils was highlighted, and particularly in geography and history for special children, including the exceptionally able' (NCC, 1993).

National Curriculum Geography, Special Needs and the Working Group

When planning the National Curriculum the Geography Working Group was concerned that children of all needs would have *access* to this area. They expressed agreement with the philosophy of the Education Reform Act of 1988 that *every* child has a right to benefit from experiences in geography and were hopeful that it would not be necessary to 'suspend or modify the recommended curriculum' too often whilst recognising that this would at times be inevitable. However, the Working Group found it difficult to express Statements of Attainment and Programmes of Study in such a way that pupils were excluded as little as possible but recommended in particular:

    (a) pupils unable to communicate by speech may use the most effective or appropriate method available to them;

    (b) pupils unable to see well enough to read or to use maps may use braille and tactile maps;

    (c) pupils who because of visual impairment or physical disability, have restricted mobility or have not developed normal concepts of space, distance or contour, may be given assistance to engage in fieldwork and fieldwork tasks within safe limits of their capabilities; and,

    (d) pupils who depend on the use of technological aids to produce graphical or written work should be enabled to do so. (Geography Working Group, Final Report, 1990)

The children with challenging and disturbed behaviour are perhaps the most difficult to be taught and assessed, whether they are in special units or are in mainstream schools. In the past in order to cope with these children, who affected others in the classroom, they were often provided with a rather sterile curriculum based on a behavioural approach (sometimes in special units as they had been excluded). Other schools who realised the significance of providing a wide range of experiences found that behaviour was improved as a result. Again this is so in mainstream schools. Children with behavioural problems can be helped to overcome them by a planned programme of work which attempts to promote self-esteem and independence (although this is difficult to prove) through a varied and differentiated curriculum. The practical nature of geography fieldwork, for example, can provide real stimulus and excitement when provided in short, relevant and rewarding bursts, thus helping with problems such as lack of concentration or inability to deal with too much abstract thought and in developing cooperative work.

Examining the National Curriculum

Of course before the opportunities presented by the National Curriculum can be fully understood and implemented, teachers need to be confident in understanding the requirements. In all primary schools, whether for special children or not, many teachers have worried about the extent of their own subject knowledge. This applies to all areas which did not have a high profile before the introduction of a National Curriculum. Understanding what constitutes good geography and the National Curriculum requirements is therefore an initial step, followed closely by an understanding of how geography links well with other subject areas and how cross-curricular themes, skills and dimensions can be incorporated. As mentioned earlier, geography is unusual in providing so many of these links naturally. An audit of work will reveal areas of strength and weakness.

Beginning work will need a combination then of understanding geography plus detailed knowledge of the pupils' individual needs and abilities or impairments. For special children, especially those with Profound and Multiple Learning Difficulties (PMLD) or Severe Learning Difficulties (SLD) and those with sensory disabilities, different methods of communication are at the *very centre of learning* and some teachers may need to make full use of a variety of ways such as Braille, Makaton signing and symbols, facial smiles and grimaces, eye contact, body language (gross and fine motor movements), technological aids, individualised signs and gestures as well as more usual means.

Geography Programmes of Study: A Planning Framework

The Programmes of Study (PoS) provide teachers of special children with a framework around which to plan. Children with PMLD and SLD may work for a long time at Key Stage 1 levels, making slow but real progress and achievement, the content being made age-appropriate for these older special pupils.

'Enabling pupils to work on appropriate National Curriculum PoS regardless of their chronological age is an important issue in schools for pupils with severe learning difficulties. School staff should ensure that pupils are taught the most appropriate parts of the National Curriculum by reference to *their current achievements irrespective of their age*.' (NCC, 1992)

Skills and the Priority of Locality

In the PoS the importance of enquiry learning is mentioned first under Geographical Skills and this seems appropriate for all children but especially those who need special help. It is particularly relevant that:

'...work should be linked to pupil's own interests and experience and capabilities and should lead to investigations based on fieldwork and classroom activities. Much learning...should be based on different experience, practical activities and exploration of the local area.' (National Curriculum Geography, 1990).

This may be good practice in all subject areas but geography in particular supports this by *requiring* pupils to use their locality to understand and interpret – photographs, aerial photographs, maps; the physical characteristics; the human element; and environmental issues. It is particularly relevant for special children whether in school or special units to use the local locality for developing their own capabilities through direct experience and the understanding of a *small area in depth* whatever their age. An appraisal of the local locality can provide teachers with a collection of suitable ideas for activities and must be one of the first things to be tackled once the requirements of the geography document are understood.

IT Skills and Geographic Concepts

Information technology also provides opportunities for special children in the use of appropriate word processing packages linked to a concept keyboard, databases or specific programmes. Computers may be a technological aid for children with poor or underdeveloped motor skills and and can also help develop specific geographical concepts such as direction and plan view, coordinates, etc. Where fieldwork is impossible, computer simulations can provide a rich source of stimulus for language development or other form of communication. Cooperative work, problem-solving and developing social skills can all be helped through a combination of geography and IT. Again the individual need of the pupil would decide on suitability. *Mapventure/Teddy Bear's Rainy Day* (Sherston Software) are just two of many programmes produced which would aid geographical enquiry. For the most able or gifted pupil IT can be used to extend their geographical understanding and for producing their own programmes or simulations.

Photographs

The use of photographs is particularly valuable for children who are not visually impaired but who find difficulty in reading text. Learning to 'read' a photograph stimulates enquiry in an exciting and manageable way. Ground level photographs of the school, the grounds and locality can be used to spot certain features whilst out walking. They can be placed in a sequence, or can be taken by the pupils themselves as a means of recording which does not involve writing. Still photographs and videos can be used back in the classroom, giving children the opportunity to bring the world into their classroom themselves, a world which they have explored and begun to understand. Photographs will incorporate many other elements from the Programmes of Study by including local street furniture, transport, the variety of jobs, homes, shops and shopping and weather. Once photographs have been used and become firmly established it could lead on to selected photographs of unfamiliar places to compare and contrast. These will be all the easier to understand, the strategies and concepts having already been explored in a local, familiar situation. Communication skills can be developed by linking a photograph with one or two Makaton signs or symbols and sensory awareness by linking photographs with sound.

Aerial photographs have proved to be successful in enabling children with special needs to begin to understand the concept of plan view and successful work has been done with secondary aged slow learners (Harwood, 1984). They have progressed through the stages of oblique and vertical aerial photographs to a better understanding of large-scale maps and then on to smaller scale. Oblique photographs progressing from near to further away are less abstract than vertical and are recognisable as a representation of reality. A vertical photograph and a map are more abstract, being in plan view and therefore more difficult, but the gradual progressive steps, beginning with ground level, on to oblique and vertical, etc, enable slow learners to achieve a greater understanding. For children lucky enough to have a high vantage point near school, aerial photographs become a valuable secondary source to complement fieldwork.

Places

The aims of place study are to make children aware of their own locality and other places, and to make comparisons, looking especially at similarities as well as differences. Becoming familiar with a locality may take longer for children who do not live there. Pupils who travel from a wide area to a special school may need to spend more time discovering this locality than those who live nearby. Once their school locality has been used to develop understanding a contrasting locality in the U.K., common to all children, can be found. This locality should provide geographical features and activities not previously studied but for children who need the concrete experience of a place it is advisable to choose a contrasting one which is close enough to visit and compare. (Even within a town or city contrast can be found in a school locality in the outer suburbs and one in the city centre) Organising field trips becomes easier the more they are experienced both by staff and pupils. Special schools have greater individual pupil needs to cater for but may have the advantage of extra staff, maybe a minibus and fewer pupils. The development of 'twinning' – where two schools exchange information, resources and offer fieldwork and visits to each other – would be beneficial in providing regular contact for special children in a contrasting locality.

Although distant places may not be regarded as suitable for children who find abstract concepts difficult or impossible to deal with, it would be interesting to discover what messages or images, if any, these pupils receive from the media especially from television. They are being made aware all the time of events in other places, concerning other people. More and more children are visiting Europe for holidays so will actually have some personal experience upon which to build. Examining places in Europe through a locality study or through a European 'dimension' would widen special children's experience. Once children have been used to looking at primary and secondary sources in their own locality through fieldwork, photographs, video, maps and other materials, the jump to looking for comparison at secondary sources about distance places could then be feasible. Real attempts can be made to see if work is possible in this area, without however making tokenistic gestures. This is where the teacher's intimate knowledge of special children becomes vital. Certainly some children with PMLD will prove difficult to access in terms of exactly how much has been understood if their difficulties in communication are huge. Their enjoyment of work, however, can often be discerned by teachers who know how to interpret a glance or gesture.

Themes: Human Geography, a Base for PSE

Many activities can be planned in the local area which help pupils to begin to be aware of houses and homes, shops, occupations, journeys, transport, the physical features and some environmental issues. In fact the human geography has strong links with the Personal and Social activities so strongly developed for special children in the past and it is in this area which teachers of special children may have excelled without realising that their work was closely related to geography. A few examples of this could be: finding a way round school, going to the local shops, buying something, experiencing different forms of transport and being able to travel alone. These are all some activities which pupils with SLD may eventually experience and are closely linked to geographical enquiry.

Work in geography can be through various media for the actual experience and the recording. Experience in the locality can be extended by photographs, video, people who live and work there talking to pupils, and by story. Role play drama, model-making, drawing, using a database, word processor, concept keyboard are all known and used ways of developing and recording ideas. This variety provides ways in which to interest pupils and help many problems faced by the teacher of special needs children.

Case Studies

These studies were provided by a small special school catering for pupils with Severe Learning Difficulties (SLD) and with Profound and Multiple Learning Difficulties (PLMD). The school has 22 children, 4 teachers, 4 nursery nurses plus the headteacher. The selections of work were undertaken by pupils whose ages ranged from 4-19 and who had very varied needs and impairments. Work was planned to begin in the school building and progress to the school grounds and the locality. Lack of space allows only a few selections but work continued into a contrasting locality and plans for studying a European locality are currently being implemented.

SPECIAL EDUCATIONAL NEEDS AND GEOGRAPHY
Example 1

Aim: to extend children's knowledge about their own locality.

Objective: to enable children to develop ideas of similarity and difference in housing, vegetation, industry, etc.

Observation: direct and photographs.

SLD children: sign/word communication.

Activity	Geographical Concepts
— To look at enlarged photo of school from the front.	
— Enquiry – What can you see? What is this? Where is it? What is it made of?	Similarity and difference.
How do we use it? Whose room is this?	Location.
— To look at line drawing of school, ask questions to identify features – discussion of features.	Sense of place
— Further features from direct experience of area.	Distance.
— Viewing all school from outside.	Continuity and change.
— Looking further out of school, pointing, naming.	

Further work
Identify all features/colour.
Classify building materials.
Looking at houses.
Picture 2 (different view overlooking school) same format.

National Curriculum Contribution, geography		S.E.N. & Cross-curricular Aspects
Former AT	*Levels*	*English/Communications.*
1	1,2	Maths. Sensori-motor.
2	1,2	Science.
3	1	Art.
4	1	History.
5	1	Personal and Social Education.

Use of School Photographs

A – Start observing school from the top of the steps
(as on photograph, safe place for discussion).
B – Look at photograph, compare with reality.
C – Look at line drawing, compare with photograph and reality. Adult
labels what child names/signs.

Questions/Pointers	Guided Process
Where are we?	
What can you see?	Observations.
What can you hear?	
Show me...	Directed observations.
What is this?	
Whose room is this?	
What part of houses	Detailed descriptions.
can you see?	
What is this?	
(sky, building, ground).	
What do you like about... ?	
Can you take me to...?	Personal responses.
(point on photo/line drawing).	

Pupils stood in an elevated place in front of school from which they could look at the school building and also see beyond to houses, other buildings and trees in the locality (Figure 13.1). The second position was similarly placed but a different view of school. Photographs of both places were used during and after the fieldwork. Recording was teacher-aided through signing and word communication showing positive understanding (in varying degrees) of features of the school and locality beyond and an ability to understand real situations represented on photographs. The pupils noticed changes which had taken place since the introductory photographs had been taken, flowers had gone, leaves were on the ground not on the trees, windows had been painted and the design on a door changed. Emphasis was laid on concentration, memory skills and working cooperatively in a group.

Further work took the pupils outside school to look at houses in the locality and whilst looking at various types and styles they used line drawings again to focus their attention on doors and windows. A door survey gave the pupils the opportunity to notice the different colours, whether there was a letterbox or not and where it was placed, the presence or absence of a bell and finally whether the pupil liked it or not, with their reasons. Other activities included the number and shape of windows, the type of glass, were there curtains or blinds and then the

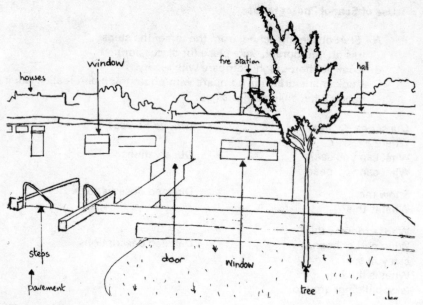

Figure 13.1

shape of the roof, the shape of slates and any pattern made, other materials used in building and the need for pipes on the outside of the house. A chart of findings was produced.

Before pupils were able to experience the following activity (Example 2, page 183) an independence programme had been undertaken where memory, safety and communication skills were developed and strengthened. Pupils had not been shopping from school before but their confidence had been developed over a period of time. Each pupil had individual strengths – for example, one was good at finding his way, another had two or three words of language, another pupil was quite chatty and another was very independent. As a group they helped each other although two adults accompanied the seven pupils, keeping in the backround as much as possible.

As an introduction to this work the pupils used photographs, discussion and samples of fruit, for a pre-activity simulation. The shopkeepers in the local shops visited knew the pupils, and the teacher had previously been to explain the work. The shopkeepers were aware that signing and gestures would be ways of communicating for some pupils. Photographs of the shops with the shopkeeper were taken and used back in the classroom for follow-up work. Signs used to support questioning for the visit were as indicated (Figure 13.2 (and then Figure 13.3)).

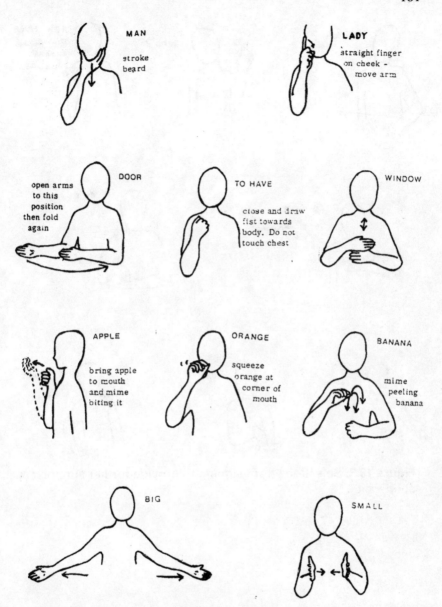

Figure 13.2: Signing to support shop visit

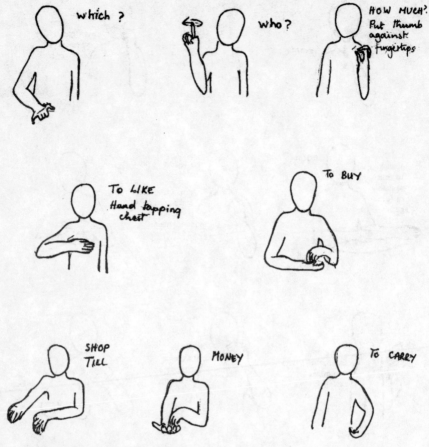

Figure 13.3: Selections from signing to provide further support for shop visit

SPECIAL EDUCATIONAL NEEDS AND GEOGRAPHY
Example 2

Aim: to show increasing knowledge and understanding of shopping activities (economic activity).

Objective: to go to shops – purchase an item by self from correct shop.

Walk to shops: to work on recognition of greengrocers' and butchers' shops.

SLD young adults: independence/life skills

Activity	Geographical Concepts
— Go to shop area with adult.	Location.
— Identify correct shops.	
— Choose item to buy.	Sense of place.
— Take money and enter.	
— Make purchase and leave shop by self. (adult to remain visible outside)	Human activities.

Follow up
What liked/not liked about activity.
What to buy next time – list
Photographs – back up (also used as pre-activity resource).

National Curriculum Contribution, Geography		S.E.N. & possible Cross-curricular Aspects
Former AT	*Levels*	*English.*
1	1,2	Communication.
2	1,2	Maths.
4	1,2	Science.
		History.
		Developmental Curriculum
		Independence/life skills
		Personal and social.

A sensory curriculum

For all children development of the senses is both important and enjoyable but for pupils with sensory impairment it is essential. In most primary schools development of all the senses takes place but few children need the emphasis which is necessary for special children. Pupils who have an impairment need as many sensory clues as possible in order to make sense of the world and in this instance the curriculum, but also to be able to communicate more fully. The geography curriculum can play a part in this. Visits to different places will provide a variety of sounds which can be recorded and used in the classroom for discussion, in games or simulations. A walk around school, along the street, a visit to the park, the seaside or into town will provide sounds to encourage good listening skills and evoke memories of a place. Many visual stimuli are available through activities mentioned earlier, i.e. fieldwork, photographs, video.

Sensory games

1 Tape noises in the classroom – discuss with pupils.

2 Take the pupils to another place to listen, tape the sounds, discuss, make the sounds.

3 Collect photographs of certain activities which produce noises relevant to one particular place or idea – for example different noises around school, in the playground, dining room, hall, etc. Tape the noises and play them back to the children who have to identify the correct photograph. This can be done with an adult, cooperatively with another child or as a game. After the school-based activities, go further afield and collect more sound/photograph combinations, related to specific places, park noises, seashore noises, noises in town or on a busy street, etc.

4 Some pupils would benefit from feeling and smelling objects, i.e. smooth pebbles from the beach, slippery seaweed, shells, sand, driftwood, etc. The taste of ice-cream, the simulated warmth of the sun, may be reminiscent of a day at the seaside and help pupils to an understanding of place alongside the sound of waves, seagulls crying and various visual images of coasts.

5 Developing sensory trails round school is an activity in which pupils can participate in making as well as enjoying – such as planting shrubs, trees and flowers to make a fragrance trail or feeling textures of walls, bark, cobbles, grass, windows.

A sensory curriculum is not new in special schools (Longhorn, 1988) and indeed is regarded only as one important aspect, amongst others, of a well-balanced whole curriculum which aims to meet the needs of individual pupils. It does provide an interesting vehicle for interpreting the geography curriculum and gives added experience of the links between people, their senses and different places.

Conclusion

In schools where there is both a SENs coordinator and a geography coordinator the task of understanding the geography requirements and providing for all children with special needs can be jointly undertaken with the class teacher of the pupil concerned. All staff, as in other areas, need to know about and be involved in decisions taken and given support to access geography. It will prove more complex in special schools where there is no geography coordinator but a way of coping may be to link with another school or cluster of schools to provide mutual support and perhaps to share expertise.

The special needs of certain children in school puts very great emphasis on teachers being thoroughly aware of and confident about the 'whole curriculum'. All aspects need to be regarded as 'resources' from which to excite and develop children's learning. Geography is one of these resources which by its practical, local-based beginning is particularly suitable for children with special needs, providing a richness of concrete experiences which promotes superior learning. Many geographically-based topics offer relevant learning situations where opportunities for rehearsal, repetition and consolidation can take place whilst maintaining interest and motivation. These are especially important factors for special children.

As a subject it has the added bonus of presenting an enormous wealth of knowledge and of developing learning through an ever-increasing circle from national to global dimensions and so subscribing in exciting ways to provision for all children in some particular way.

REFERENCES

E. Adams and C. Ward (1982) *Art and the Built Environment: a Teacher's Approach* (London: Longman/Schools Council).

J. and A. Ahlberg (1978) *Each Peach, Pear Plum* (Edinburgh: Oliver and Boyd).

L. and A. Ahlberg (1987) *The Clothes Horse and Other Stories* (London: Viking Kestrel).

R. Alexander (1984) *Primary Teaching* (London: Holt, Rinehart and Winston).

R. Alexander (1989) 'Core subjects and autumn leaves: the National Curriculum and languages of primary education', *Education 3–13*, **17**, pp.3–8.

M. Anno (1975) *Anno's Counting Book* (London: Macmillan).

A. B. Archer and H. Thomas (1936) *Geography: First Series: Book 1 – Six Children of Faraway Lands* (London: Ginn and Co.).

R. Austin (1990) *Communicating across Europe* (Belfast: European Studies Project).

D. P. Ausubel (1968) *Educational Psychology: a Cognitive View* (New York: Rinehart and Winston).

P. Bailey (1991) *Securing a Place for Geography in the National Curriculum of English and Welsh Schools: a Study in the Politics and Practicalities of Curriculum Reform* (Sheffield: The Geographical Association/Leicester University Geography Department).

P. Bailey and T. Binns (eds) (1987) *A Case for Geography* (Sheffield: The Geographical Association).

J. Baker (1989) *Where the Forest Meets the Sea* (London: Walker Books).

J. Baker (1992) *Window* (London: Random House).

K. Baker (1987) The National Curriculum: *Key to Better Standards*, Speech of Secretary of State for Education, University of Manchester, 17 September.

D. Balderstone and D. Lambert (eds) (1992) *Assessment Matters* (Sheffield: The Geographical Association).

R. Beddis and C. Mares (1988) *School Links International: a New Approach to Primary School Linking round the World* (Bristol: Avon County Council/London: World Wildlife Fund).

G. H. Bell (1991) *Developing a European Dimension in Primary Schools* (London: David Fulton Publishers).

G. H. Bell and R. Dransfield (1992) *Teaching about Europe* (London: Shell Education Service).

R. B. Bennett (1992) 'Motor cars', in A. Owen (ed) *Pigeons and Other City Poems* (London: Macmillan).

B. Bernstein (1975) *Class, Codes and Control – Towards a Theory of Educational Transmissions* (London: Routledge and Kegan Paul).

A. Bilham-Boult (1988) *Using Computers in Fieldwork* (Coventry: Micro-electronics Education Support Unit (MESU)).

J. M. Blaut (1991) 'Natural Mapping', *Transactions of the Institute of British Geographers*, **16**, pp.55–74.

W. A. L. Blyth, K. R. Cooper, R. Derricott, G. Elliott, H. Sumner and A. Waplington (1976) *Place, Time and Society 8–13: Curriculum Planning in History, Geography and Social Science* (London: Collins/Bristol: ESL).

W. A. L. Blyth and R. Derricott (1977) *The Social Significance of Middle Schools* (London: Batsford).

W. A. L. Blyth (1990) *Making the Grade for Primary Humanities* (Milton Keynes:

Open University Press).

Board of Education (1931) *Report of the Consultative Committee on the Primary School* (Hadow Report), (London: HMSO).

D. Boardman (1983) *Graphicacy and Geography Teaching* (London: Croom Helm).

A. and R. Bonner (1982) *Summerwords* (London: Abelard-Schuman).

R. Bowles (1993) *Resources for Key Stages 1, 2 and 3* (Sheffield: The Geographical Association).

W. L. Brittain (1979) *Creativity, Art and the Young Child* (London: Collier Macmillan).

E. Brough (1983) 'Geography through Art', in J. Huckle (ed) *Geographical Education: Reflection and Action* (Oxford: Oxford University Press), pp.56–63.

S. Catling (1978) 'Cognitive Mapping Exercises as a Primary Geographical Experience', *Teaching Geography*, **3**, pp.120–3.

S. Catling (1984) 'Building Less Able Children's Map Skills', *Remedial Education*, **19**, pp.21–7; also in J. Dilkes and A. Nicholls (eds) (1988) *Low Attainers and the Teaching of Geography* (Sheffield: The Geographical Association), pp.25–28.

S. Catling (1985) 'Mapwork', in G. Corney and E. Rawling (eds) *Teaching Slow Learners through Geography* (Sheffield: The Geographical Association), pp.54–66.

Central Advisory Council for Education (England) (1967) *Children and their Primary Schools* (The Plowden Report), 2 vols. (London: HMSO).

Central Bureau (1991) *Making the Most of your Partner School Abroad* (London: Central Bureau for Educational Visits and Exchanges).

Central Bureau (1993) *The European Dimension in Education* (London: Central Bureau for Educational Visits and Exchanges).

Central Bureau (1993) *Resources for Teaching about Europe* (London: Central Bureau for Educational Visits and Exchanges).

D. and W. Clempson (1991) *The Really Practical Guide to Primary Assessment* (London: Stanley Thornes).

C. Conner (1990) 'National Curriculum assessment and the primary school: reactions and illustrations of emerging practice, *The Curriculum Journal*, **1**, pp.139–154.

G. C. Cons and C. Fletcher (1938) *Actuality in Schools: an Experiment in Social Education* (London: Methuen).

Council for Cultural Cooperation (1993) *An Intercultural Approach to School Links and Exchanges* (London: Council for Cultural Cooperation).

H. Cowcher (1991) *Antarctica* (London: Picture Corgi).

H. Cowcher (1991) *Rainforest* (London: Picture Corgi).

P. Croft (1993) 'Experiencing geography, *Special Education*, **69**, insert.

K. Crossley-Holland (1978) 'A beach of stones' in C. Causley (ed) *The Puffin Book of Salt Sea Verse* (London: Puffin).

Curriculum Council for Wales (1991) *Geography in the National Curriculum: Non-Statutory Guidance for Teachers* (Cardiff: Curriculum Council for Wales).

Curriculum Council for Wales (1992) *Environmental Education: a Framework for the Development of a Cross-curricular Theme*, Advisory Paper 17 (Cardiff: CCW).

R. Daugherty (ed) (1989) *Geography in the National Curriculum* (Sheffield: The Geographical Association).

J. Davidson and J. Krause (eds) (1992) *Geography, IT and the National Curriculum* (Sheffield: The Geographical Association).

Department of Education and Science (1967) *Children and their Primary Schools, Vol.1* (London: HMSO).

Department of Education and Science (1978) *Primary Education in England: a Survey by HM Inspectors of Schools* (London: HMSO).

Department of Education and Science (1983) *9–13 Middle Schools: An Illustrative Survey* (London: HMSO).

Department of Education and Science (1985) *Education 8–12 in Combined and Middle Schools* (London: HMSO).

Department of Education and Science (1989) *Aspects of Primary Education: the Teaching and Learning of History and Geography* (London: HMSO).

Department of Education and Science (1989) *Personal and Social Education from 5 to 16: Curriculum Matters 14 – an HMI Series* (London: HMSO).

Department of Education and Science (1989) *Environmental Education from 5 to 16: Curriculum Matters 13 – an HMI Series* (London: HMSO).

Department of Education and Science (1989) *Her Majesty's Inspectorate: Aspects of Primary Education: The Teaching and Learning of History and Geography* (London: HMSO).

Department of Education and Science and the Welsh Office (1989) *National Curriculum Geography Working Group: Interim Report* (London: DES).

Department of Education and Science and the Welsh Office (1990) *Geography for Ages 5 to 16* (London: DES).

Department of Education and Science (1991) *Geography in the National Curriculum* (London: HMSO).

Department for Education (1992) *Policy Models: a Guide to Developing and Implementing European Dimension Policies in Schools* (London: DfE).

R. Derricott and W. A. L. Blyth (1979) *Cognitive Development: the Social Dimension*, in A. Floyd (ed) *Cognitive Development in the School Years* (London: Croom Helm and the Open University Press).

R. Derricott (ed) (1985) *Curriculum Continuity – Primary to Secondary* (Windsor: NFER-Nelson).

J. Dewey (1916) *Democracy and Education: an Introduction to the Philosophy of Education* (New York: The Free Press).

P. Dupasquier (1988) *Our House on the Hill* (London: Puffin).

P. Dupasquier (1984) *The Railway Station* (London: Walker Books).

P. Dupasquier (1986) *Dear Daddy* (London: Walker Books).

G. Elliott (1979) *Teaching for Concepts* (London: Collins/Bristol: ESL).

J. Findall (1990) *The Journey Home* (London: Walker Books).

D. Finlow (1993) 'Experiencing geography', *Special Education*, **69**, insert.

M. Foreman (1984) *Dinosaurs and all that Rubbish* (London: Puffin).

M. Foreman (1992) *One World* (London: Red Fox).

S. Freundschuh (1990) 'Can children use maps to navigate?', *Cartographica*, **27**, pp.54–66.

A. Gadsden (1991) *Geography and History through Stories* (Sheffield: The Geographical Association).

O. Garnett (1934) *Fundamentals in School Geography: a Book for Teachers and Students in Training* (London: Harrap).

O. Garnett (1940) 'Reality in geography', *The Journal of Education*, **72**, pp.171–3.

J. George (1968) *My Side of the Mountain* (London: Puffin).

N. J. Graves and M. Naish (eds) (1986) *Profiling in Geography* (Sheffield: The Geographical Association).

N. Gray and P. Dupasquier (1990) *A Country Far Away* (London: Puffin).

A. Grifalconi (1989) *The Village of Round and Square Houses* (London: Picturemac).

Hansard, *Debate on the Crowther Report* (March 1960).

W. Harlen, C. Gipps, P. Broadfoot, and D. Nuttall (1992) 'Assessment and the improvement of education', *The Curriculum Journal*, **3**, pp.215–230.

D. Harwood (1984) 'Introducing mapwork to ESN(M) children through using aerial photographs', *Remedial Education*, **19**, pp.65–72.

M. Hedderwick (1986) *Katie Morag Delivers the Mail* (London: Picture Lions).

G. Hickman (1950) 'Sample studies: a method and its limitations', *Journal of Geography*, **49**, pp.151–9.

P. H. Hirst (1975) *Knowledge and the Curriculum* (London: Routledge and Kegan Paul).

D. Horner and J. Lincoln (1993) *Whose Story is it Anyway?* (Winsford, Woodford Lodge: Cheshire Oracy Project and Arts in a Multi-cultural Society).

P. Howard (1979) 'Art, design and landscape: some practical ideas, *Teaching Geography*, **5**, pp.84–6,

S. Hughes (1986) *Lucy and Tom at the Seaside* (London: Picture Corgi).

R. Isadora (1993) *At the Crossroads* (London: Red Fox).

S. Jex (1979) 'Urban field studies in a primary school', *Teaching Geography*, **4**, pp.148–52.

H. B. Joicey (1986) *An Eye on the Environment: an Art Education Project* (London: World Wildlife Fund/Bell and Hyman).

G. Kaye (1990) *Summer in Small Street* (London: Mammoth).

W. A. Kent (1992) 'The new technology and geographical education', in M. C. Naish (ed) *Geography and Education: National and International Perspectives* (London: Institute of Education, University of London).

W. A. Kent (ed) (1992) 'IT and geography in the National Curriculum: some initial reactions', *Journal of Computer Assisted Learning*, **8**, pp.2–15.

D. Lambert (ed) (1990) *Teacher Assessment and National Curriculum Geography* (Sheffield: The Geographical Association).

S. Leigh (1990) *Journey to the Lost Temple* (London: Usborne).

A. Lewis (1991) *Primary Special Needs and the National Curriculum* (London: Routledge).

S. Limb (1988) *Trees Rule OK* (London: Orchard Books).

P. Lively (1981) *The Revenge of Samuel Stokes* (London: Puffin).

F. Longhorn (1988) *A Sensory Curriculum for Very Special Children* (London: Souvenir Press).

R. A. Manzer (1970) *Teachers and Politics: The Role of the National Union of Teachers in the Making of National Education Policy in England and Wales since 1944* (Manchester: Manchester University Press).

S. Marshall (1963) *An Experiment in Education* (Cambridge University Press).

G. C. Martin and K. Wheeler (1975) *Insights into Environmental Education* (Edinburgh: Oliver and Boyd).

J. R. Martland and S. E. Walsh (1993) *Developing Navigational Skills: Using the Silva Model 7DNS Compass* (London: National Coaching Foundation, Sports Council).

T. Masterton (1969) *Environmental Studies: a Concentric Approach* (Edinburgh: Oliver and Boyd).

H. Mellar and A. Jackson (1992) 'IT in post-graduate teacher training', *Journal of Computer Assisted Learning*, **8**, pp.231–243.

D. Mills (ed) (1988) *Geographical Work in Primary and Middle Schools* (Sheffield:

190

The Geographical Association), Chapters 7 and 10.

Ministry of Education (1964) *Report on the Working Party of the Schools' Curricula and Examinations* (London: HMSO).

Y. Moore and J. Bannatyne-Cugnet (1992) *A Prairie Alphabet* (Montreal, Canada: Tundra Books).

S. Morgan (1990) *Mother and Daughter: the Story of Daisy and Gladys Corunna* (Fremantle: Arts Centre Press, South Fremantle, Australia).

E. Moss (1985) *Picture Books for Young People* (Stroud: Thimble Press).

G. Muller (1989) *A Garden in the City* (London: Macdonald).

D. Murray (1992) 'IT capability in primary schools – a case of something lost in the translation?', *Journal of Computer Assisted Learning*, **8**, pp.96–103.

M. C. Naish (ed) (1992) *Primary Schools, Geography and the National Curriculum in England* (Sheffield: The Geographical Association).

National Council for Educational Technology (1989) *Learning Geography with Computers* (Coventry: NCET).

National Council for Educational Technology (1991) *Focus on IT* (Coventry: NCET).

National Council for Educational Technology (1991) *Making IT happen: Issues for Policy makers. Occasional Paper 4* (Coventry: NCET).

National Council for Educational Technology (1992) *Making Links* (Coventry: NCET).

National Council for Educational Technology (1993) *Portable Computers in Initial Teacher Education* (Coventry: NCET).

National Council for Educational Technology (1993) *Project INTENT. The Final Report* (Coventry: NCET).

National Council for Educational Technology (1993) *The Future Curriculum with IT: Seminar report* (Coventry: NCET).

National Curriculum Council (1991) *Non-Statutory Guidance: Geography* (York: NCC).

National Curriculum Council (1991) *Non-Statutory Guidance: Information Technology Capability* (York: NCC).

National Curriculum Council (1992) *Planning for Key Stage 2: Trial Version* (York: NCC).

National Curriculum Council (1993) *The National Curriculum and its Assessment: an Interim Report (Dearing)* (York: NCC).

National Curriculum Council (1993) *The National Curriculum at Key Stages 1 and 2* (York: NCC).

National Curriculum Council (1990) *Curriculum Guidance 3: The Whole Curriculum* (York: NCC).

National Curriculum Council (1988) *English for Ages 5 to 16* (York: NCC).

National Curriculum Council (1990) *Curriculum Guidance 4: Education for Economic and Industrial Understanding* (York: NCC).

National Curriculum Council (1990) *Curriculum Guidance 7: Environmental Education* (York: NCC).

National Curriculum Council (1990) *Curriculum Guidance 8: Education for Citizenship* (York: NCC).

National Curriculum Council (1992) *Curriculum Guidance 9: The National Curriculum and Pupils with Severe Learning Difficulties* (York: NCC).

National Curriculum Council (1993) *Special Needs and the National Curriculum: Opportunity and Challenge* (York: NCC).

D. J. Nias (1985) 'Hinge or bracket? middle school teachers' views of continuity at 11', in R. Derricott (ed) *Curriculum Continuity – Primary to Secondary* (Windsor: NFER/Nelson), pp.101–117.

H. N. Nicholson (1991) *Geography and History in the National Curriculum* (Sheffield: The Geographical Association).

Office for Standards in Education (1993) *Curriculum Organisation and Classroom Practice in Primary Schools: a Follow-up Report* (London: OFSTED).

S. O'Huigin (1985) *Atmosfear* (Windsor, Ontario: Black Moss Press).

P. Oleghe (1978) 'A sudden storm', in N. Machin (ed) *African Poetry for Schools* (London: Longman).

T. Ottosson (1988) 'What does it take to read a map?', *Cartographica*, **25**, pp.28–35.

G. Owen (1992) 'Our school', in J. Tuckey (ed) *Verse Universe* (London: BBC).

C. Parker and A. Tapsfield (eds) (1989) *Geography Through Topics in Middle and Primary Schools (including applications of IT)* (Sheffield: The Geographical Association).

J. Paton-Walsh (1992) *Babylon* (London: Red Fox).

R. S. Peters (ed) (1969) *Perspectives on Plowden* (London: Routledge and Kegan Paul).

J. Piaget and B. Inhelder (1956) *The Child's Conception of Space* (London: Routledge and Kegan Paul).

W. Pick and M. Renwick (1986) 'Teaching the less able student in geography', in J. Fien, R. Gerber and P. Wilson (eds) *The Geography Teacher's Guide to the Classroom* (Melbourne: Macmillan Company of Australia), pp.208–225.

M. Plaskow (ed) (1985) *Life and Death of the Schools Council* (London: The Falmer Press).

W. Plomer (1986) 'The Victoria Falls', in R. Jones (ed) *One World Poets* (London: Heinemann).

N Procter (1991) 'Geography for pupils with special educational needs', in N. Jones and J. W. Docking (eds) *Special Educational Needs and the Education Reform Act* (London: Trentham Books), pp.101–115.

D. Riley (1992) 'Geography curricula and IT resource implications', in W. A. Kent (ed) *IT and Geography in the National Curriculum. Some Initial Reactions, Journal of Computer Assisted Learning*, **8**, pp.2–15.

M. Rudd (1980) 'Thematic town trails: a Method of Approach', *Teaching Geography*, **5**, pp.126–8.

R. Savage (1992) *School Links and Exchanges in Europe* (London: Council for Cultural Cooperation).

P. Schebesta (1993) *Among Congo Pygmies* (London: Hutchison), quoted in T. Pickles (1934) *Africa* (London: Dent and Sons), pp.65–6.

S. Scoffham and T. Jewson (1993) 'Geography through Fairy Tales', *Primary Geographer*, **12**, p.2.

School Curriculum and Assessment Authority (1993) *The National Curriculum and its Assessment (The Dearing Report)* (London: SCAA).

School Examinations and Assessment Council (1993) *Geography Standard Assessment Tasks: Teacher's Handbook* (London: SEAC).

School Examinations and Assessment Council (1993) *Children's Work Assessed: Geography and History, Key Stage 1* (London: SEAC).

School Examinations and Assessment Council (1993) *Standard Assessment Tasks: Geography, Teacher's Pack* (London: SEAC).

Schools Council (1969) *The Middle Years of Schooling. From 9 to 13*, Working Paper No. 22 (London: HMSO).

Schools Council (1974) *Children's Growth through Creative Experince: Art and Craft Education 8–13* (London: Schools Council/Van Nostrand Reinhold Company).

R. Scruton (ed) (1991) *Conservative Texts: an Anthology* (Basingstoke: Macmillan).

J. Sebba (1991) *Planning Geography for Pupils with Special Learning Difficulties* (Sheffield: The Geographical Association).

J. Sebba and J. Clarke (1991) 'Meeting the needs of pupils within history and geography', in R. Ashdown, B. Carpenter and K. Bovair (eds) *The Curriculum Challenge* (London: The Falmer Press), pp.117–140.

J. and S. Snape (1990) *Giant* (London: Walker Books).

C. P. Spencer, M. Blades and K. Morsley (1989) *The Child in the Physical Environment* (Chichester: Wiley).

L. D. and E. C. Stamp (1930) *The New Age Geographies: Junior Series* (London: Longmans Green and Co.).

C. Thiele (1986) *Storm Boy and Other Stories* (Sydney, Australia: Weldon Publishing).

H. G. Thomas (1937) *Teaching Geography* (London: Ginn and Co.)

C. F. Tunnicliffe (1942) *My Country Book* (London: The Studio).

A. R. Van der Loeff (1963) *Children on the Oregon Trail* (London: Puffin).

S. Van Rose (1992) *Volcano: Eye Witness Guide No. 38* (London: Dorling Kindersley).

S. E. Walsh, J. R. Martland and R. R. Stewart (1991) 'The map orientation skills of young children – a preliminary investigation', *Scientific Journal of Orienteering*, **1/2**, pp.90–103.

S. E. Walsh and J. R. Martland (1993) 'The orientation and navigational skills of young children – an application of two intervention strategies', *The Journal of Navigation*, **46**, pp.63–68.

C. Ward and A. Fyson (1973) *Streetwork: the Exploding School* (London: Routledge and Kegan Paul).

H. Warner (1990) 'LOGO and geography', *Journal of Computer Assisted Learning*, **6**, pp.202–216.

D. Warwick (ed) (1973) *Integrated Studies in the Secondary School* (London: Routledge and Kegan Paul).

D. Watson (1993) *Development of IT and Geography in the School Curriculum: Problems and Possibilities* (Unpublished paper written for DfE Conference).

D. Watts (ed) (1993) *The Impact Report. An evaluation of the impact of Information Technology on children's achievements in primary and secondary schools* (London: Kings College).

S. Weatherill (1990) *Lucy's Year* (London: Two-Can Publishing).

P. Wild and K. Hodgkinson (1992) 'IT capability in primary initial teacher training', *Journal of Computer Assisted Learning*, **8**, pp.79–89.

D. Wright (1993) '"Colourful South Africa"? an analysis of text-book images', *Multiracial Education*, **10**, pp.27–36.

T. Wright (1989) 'High on the hill', in R. Wilson (ed) *Out and About: Poems of the Outdoors* (London: Puffin).

P. Young and C. Tyre (1992) *Gifted or Able: Realising Children's Potential* (Milton Keynes: Open University Press).

INDEX